THE
WEDDING
POCKET BIBLE

THE
WEDDING
POCKET BIBLE

CATHY HOWES

First edition published in Great Britain in 2010 by
Crimson Publishing, a division of Crimson Business Ltd.
This reprint first published in Great Britain in 2021 by Crimson
An imprint of Hodder & Stoughton
An Hachette UK company

2

A CIP catalogue record for this title is available from the British Library

Paperback ISBN 978 190708 708 0

Printed and bound in Great Britain by Clays Ltd, Elcograf S.p.A.

Hodder & Stoughton policy is to use papers that are natural, renewable
and recyclable products and made from wood grown in sustainable
forests. The logging and manufacturing processes are expected to
conform to the environmental regulations of the country of origin.

Hodder & Stoughton Ltd
Carmelite House
50 Victoria Embankment
London EC4Y 0DZ

www.hodder.co.uk

CONTENTS

INTRODUCTION

Love does not consist of gazing at each other, but in looking together in the same direction.
Antoine de Saint-Exupéry, French writer 1900-1944

A wedding is fundamentally about two people promising to love each other for the rest of their lives. It's a simple enough premise you'd think, but it's one that has evolved through the centuries from a simple celebration steeped in tradition and superstition to an industry worth billions of pounds a year in the UK. It's not for nothing the term 'bridezilla' came in to common usage to describe the frantic, frazzled, often competitive bride-to-be who doesn't know her ranunculus from her recessional and feels like she's run several marathons by the time she reaches the moment she says her vows.

If you are that frazzled bride-to-be (or you're engaged to her!) this book doesn't set out to tell you how to get married, what colour schemes to use or how many bridesmaids you should have – they are your decisions and you should have fun with them – it's about collecting together all the facts, traditions, trends and tips that can help you make those decisions, give you food for thought, inspiring ideas and, frankly, a laugh now and then. There are Stress Buster tips for when the pressure gets a bit much, Money Saver tips with suggestions for how you can trim your budget and plenty of snippets of 'wedformation' which are not things you have to do, but guidelines that might smooth your journey to the big day when you say 'I do'.

This book is here to help you understand the ins and outs of a wedding, and offer you a handy reference for you to check the basic information at each step so that you're free to focus on all the details to make your wedding truly special.

CONGRATULATIONS! YOU'RE ENGAGED

Congratulations you've decided to get married. You've made the decision to devote your life to someone else. That's the easy part, now you have to plan your wedding. This chapter looks at the first steps you should take, gives you some background information on what it means to be engaged and how you can celebrate and share your news with your loved ones.

 ENGAGEMENTS THROUGHOUT HISTORY

ENGAGEMENTS AS A BUSINESS TRANSACTION

Back in the dark days of the Anglo-Saxons, a wedding was more a secular arrangement than a religious sacrament. The girl and her young man would plight their troth and some money or land would be exchanged as part of 'the deal'. A priest might have popped along to give his blessing, but it was more a business arrangement than a romantic rite of passage. In fact the derivation of the word 'wedding' is thought to come from the Anglo-Saxon for wager – ie the groom 'betting' on a better future with the money his new bride would bring as a dowry!

Later during the heady days of serial groom King Henry VIII, boys as young as 14 and girls as young as 12 were often betrothed in marriage and it remained more of a business deal than a romantic whim. Usually betrothals were more a case of pushy parents signing land-grabbing deals and haggling over dowries than anything to do with love. Over the centuries the ages of a bride and groom crept up so that they were at least mature enough to make their own decisions. Forty years ago, in 1970, the average age of a bride was 22 and a groom was 24.

MODERN ENGAGEMENTS

Today the average age for a man to get married is 31, while his fiancée is aged between 29 and 30. In all likelihood they are also both established in their jobs, financially independent from their families and living together. And it is now the couple themselves who announce their intentions to get married to their parents, not the other way around.

Pocket fact ❧

In 2007 a former Lord Mayor of Torbay, James Mason, 93, married Peggy Clark, 84, and the couple became one of the UK's oldest newlyweds with a combined age of 177 years. James popped the question after they'd known each other for only three days. They were married a month later after agreeing that there wasn't much point in a long engagement!

🌿 ASKING DAD'S PERMISSION 🌿

I love your daughter, Jack. I love her more than anything. But frankly, sir, I'm a little terrified of being your son-in-law.
Ben Stiller, *Meet the Parents*

Some modern, independent women scoff at the idea of their boyfriend asking their dad's permission for their hand in marriage, although others still see it as a gesture of respect rather than ownership. It's one of the seemingly old fashioned traditions that many brides like to hang on to because it marks the occasion and is the first of many rites of passage associated with tying the knot.

In the film *Meet the Parents* (2000), actors Ben Stiller and Robert de Niro starred in an entire film devoted to the idea that a potential groom has to get the father-in-law's blessing before popping the question, proving the extent to which this desire to uphold tradition dominates many couples' marital plans. (For more wedding-themed movies turn to pages 28–32.)

Pocket fact &

Before proposing to Friends star Courteney Cox, traditionalist David Arquette called on her parents, Richard and Courteney, and asked their permission to marry their daughter.

❀ THE PROPOSAL ❀

With roughly 80% of women saying they were disappointed by their partner's proposal there's a lot of pressure for a man to get it right. Do you go for extravagant sky-writing, a quiet proposal over a candle-lit dinner, or something more personal like going back to the place you met? Of course there's also the option some women who are tired of waiting for their man to pop the question choose to follow: a 5th century tradition which allows women to propose on 29 February during a leap year.

However the proposal happens it will be a happy moment you will remember for the rest of your life.

The history of leap year proposals

The tradition of leap year proposals is credited to Ireland's famous St Bridget back in the 5th century. Apparently many of the nuns under St Bridget's care were keen to get married (in the days when nuns were allowed to) but proposals were a bit thin on the ground. So the redoubtable Bridget turned to Ireland's premier saint, St Patrick, for guidance and he granted the nuns permission to pop the question every four years on 29 February. (Although whether the number of weddings among the lonely nuns soared is not a matter of record!) Despite the custom that women can traditionally propose to their menfolk in a leap year, it's believed that less than 10% of proposals in the UK come from women.

Pocket fact &

In the 13th century Queen Margaret of Scotland actually passed a law which said any man who refused a proposal in a leap year would be fined — although this was often watered down from a financial penalty to just a kiss.

TEN UNUSUAL WAYS TO POP THE QUESTION

1. Tina Kilford nearly choked on her popcorn when boyfriend Tom Lane appeared on the screen at their local Cineworld in Dorset. Tom convinced the cinema staff to let him show his home-made video which saw him holding up a series of cards with lines asking her to marry him, to the tune of Joe Cocker's *You are so beautiful*.

2. Lynsey Foster was filming the Channel 4 programme *Deal or No Deal* with Noel Edmonds when boyfriend Martin Toms dashed down from the audience and asked her for her hand in marriage. Lynsey went on to win £20,000 towards their wedding in the Seychelles.

3. Rachael Smith nearly missed the proposal of marriage from boyfriend Jamie Coleman because her newsagent ran out of papers. Jamie had placed a proposal in the announcement section of *The Times*, which he knew she always read, but she was forced to buy *The Telegraph* instead and missed it until Jamie pointed out his romantic handiwork.

4. *Heartbeat* actress Tricia Penrose received her romantic proposal from husband Mark while she was relaxing in the tub, complete with candles and a bottle of wine.

5. Racing fan David Boydell sponsored a whole horserace to propose to girlfriend Wendy. He called it the 'Will You marry Me Wendy Balmain Maiden Hurdle?' and it ran at a meeting in Musselburgh, Scotland.

6. Carol Mackenzie was on her way to work with boyfriend Stuart McGowan when she spotted a crowd of people staring up at a billboard at the side of a road in Clydebank.

When Stuart pulled over on the verge she saw it was a billboard carrying the giant letters 'Carol Mackenzie will you marry me?'

7. William Dallyn wanted girlfriend Reimi Fukami to be in no doubt of how much he loved her, so he and a team of friends took three hours to write Marry Me Reimi in 15ft letters on the beach at Braunton Burrows in Devon.

8. When Colleen Brady agreed to appear on GMTV to speak to her boyfriend Warrant Officer 2nd class Nick Walker who was in Afghanistan for Christmas, she had no idea he would go down on one knee on live TV. The proposal came from his camp in Helmand Province, Afghanistan by satellite link and the tearful bride-to-be said 'yes' in front of millions of viewers.

9. Actor Jared Harris said it with flowers when he asked fellow actor Emilia Fox to be his wife. Emilia opened the bedroom door in the morning to find the whole house filled with flowers. The trail of blooms led down the stairs and out in to the garden where Jared finally proposed.

10. And one that wasn't! The newswires went into overdrive in December 2009 when repeat prankster Robbie Williams supposedly proposed to girlfriend Ayda Field live on Sydney's 2Day FM radio station. He even convinced his mother, Jan, who was allegedly spotted by the paparazzi shopping for an engagement card. The former Take That star later admitted it was just a publicity stunt.

Pocket fact

He may have spoken on the world stage many times, but when it came to proposing marriage to wife Cherie, Tony Blair seems to have forgotten who was meant to be on one knee. In a 2007 documentary Mrs Blair revealed the former PM suggested they get married out of the blue as they were preparing to leave their rented holiday property in Tuscany. She was on her knees cleaning the loo at the time!

 THE ENGAGEMENT RING

As far back as the ancient Egyptians and Romans, the unbroken circle of a ring represented eternal love. One of the earliest mentions of a ring being used as a symbol of commitment or engagement however has been traced back to a 9th century Pope, a chap called Nicolas I, who described the ring as one of many 'espousal gifts' a suitor should give to his sweetheart.

Pocket fact

Engagement and wedding bands were not always worn on the second finger of the left hand. The ancient Romans believed that the third finger had a vein that ran straight to the heart, so wearing a ring on this digit was more emotionally significant.

You don't see many of Pope Nicolas' espousal gifts at high street jewellers these days, but there are a bewildering number of choices of metals and stones for engagement rings. Custom used to dictate (or was it, as many people suspect, a clever marketing bod in the jewellery industry?) that a groom-to-be should spend at least a month's salary on an engagement ring. That's somewhere around the £2,100 mark (before tax), based on a man's average salary, although the 2009 'Cost of A Wedding' survey of 1,000 brides at youandyourwedding.co.uk revealed that they are actually spending something in the region of £1,700.

Pocket tip

Remember hands swell in summer and shrink in winter, so try any ring on in both temperatures (indoors and out, or after running under hot and cold taps) to make sure you have the right fit. And get the rings insured — one in four wedding rings are lost within five years of marriage.

WHICH METAL TO CHOOSE?

Unless the proposal came complete with a diamond sparkler in a box, most brides like to have a say in the engagement ring. It's a good idea to set a spending limit before you go, you don't want to have that conversation with the shop assistant listening. Be reasonable in your expectations and think about the type of ring you would like before you go, that way you won't be overwhelmed by all the different options.

When you go shopping for the engagement ring it's worth considering the wedding band at the same time, because the two have to sit together for a long time. Wedding bands were traditionally yellow gold, but white gold and the more expensive platinum (plus its more affordable, less weighty cousin 950 Palladium) are becoming increasingly popular. So, too, is rose gold, popular in the Edwardian age and throughout the 1920s and 1930s, and enjoying a renaissance at the moment, especially among brides looking for a vintage feel. Make sure the groom thinks about his wedding band too; traditionally wedding bands are matching rings so it makes sense to have a shared idea of what you want.

Pocket fact ✆

Gold is measured in carats — 24 carat gold is the purest form, 18 carat gold is 18 parts gold and 6 parts other metals, 9 carat gold is 9 parts gold, 9 parts other metals. By the very nature of its softness, pure gold is not usually practical for wedding bands which need to be hard-wearing.

Pocket tip 🍸

Platinum is the most hard-wearing and durable metal — it is denser than gold so would be up to 40% heavier than an identical ring made in white gold.

WHAT ARE THE FOUR CS?

These are the four standard descriptions jewellers use to classify a diamond. Unless you're an expert in fine jewellery, knowing what they mean won't necessarily help you choose the right diamond for you, but as a rule of thumb they can help nervous shoppers understand why a big stone is not necessarily the most expensive.

Clarity

The clarity refers to the number of inclusions (little markings) that can be seen inside the diamond. Obviously, the more of these inside the stone the less pure it is (and less valuable). This is why a smaller stone with a few inclusions can still be worth more than a bigger less perfect stone.

Colour

The colour of a diamond actually refers to the stone's lack of colour – the less colour it reflects the more valuable it is.

Cut

The cut is not just about making the shape of the diamond; the more surfaces (or facets) it has, the more light it reflects which makes it more of a sparkler. Popular cuts of diamonds for engage-ment rings include marquise, pear, princess, round and oval.

Carat

Carat is used to define the weight of a diamond – confusingly the same name of the measurement for gold but not to be confused with it! A diamond carat is worth approximately 0.2g, but a heavier dia-mond doesn't necessarily mean it's more valuable (see Cut, above).

Pocket fact &

The Kimberley Process is an international agreement launched in 2002 to ensure that all diamonds coming onto the market are conflict free – meaning that no injury or hardship was caused to the local population in the region where the diamonds were mined. The Process is also committed to making sure that the sale of the diamonds will not go to fund any hostile forces in war zones.

Pocket tip 🥂

Many couples now like to design their own rings, or maybe have the two wedding bands made from the same piece of gold for sentimental reasons but remember – a handmade ring is always going to be more expensive than a machine-made one.

PRECIOUS AND SEMI-PRECIOUS STONES

To get a good, flawless diamond – whatever its size – can be expensive, so a pretty and more pocket-friendly alternative is to choose precious or semi-precious stones. The term 'precious' has no bearing on the stone's value – it refers to its mineral hardness. Hard stones include sapphire, ruby and emerald and semi-precious stones include amethyst, tourmaline and topaz. Some couples choose to use the bride-to-be's birth stone in place of a diamond (although this doesn't help if you were born in April!).

Birth stones
- **January:** Garnet
- **February:** Amethyst
- **March:** Aquamarine
- **April:** Diamond
- **May:** Emerald
- **June:** Pearl
- **July:** Ruby
- **August:** Periodot
- **September:** Sapphire
- **October:** Opal
- **November:** Topaz
- **December:** Turquoise

Pocket fact 🔗

For years the bride-to-be could flash off her engagement ring while all the groom-to-be had to show for it was the receipt. Now grooms are getting in on the act too with the growing popularity of the 'mengagement' ring. Singer and actress Jennifer Hudson bought her fiancé David Otunga a $15,000 mengagement ring when they got engaged in December 2009.

❦ THE ANNOUNCEMENT ❦

At the start of the 20th century, while pioneering women were marching to gain the vote, the mission of many society debutantes was simply to bag a good husband. And when the suitor was hooked, it was all very proper to announce their engagement in the London *Times*, while less aristocratic types would settle for a modest mention in the regional press.

Today, Britain's broadsheets still offer a wedding announcement service (along with births and deaths, commonly known as the Hatch, Match and Dispatch department) and the service has, like everything else, gone online. *The Times* online publishes wedding announcements daily with a facility to send the announcement to a friend or leave your congratulations for the happy couple in cyber space. In the high-speed age of text and email though, a formal engagement announcement is still a gentle nod to a bygone age when things were 'done properly'.

Traditionally announcements were made in both national and regional press, with the bride and her family named first in papers in her home town and the groom's first in his.

In the same way that wording on invitations can vary (see pages 50–51), engagement announcements can also be formal or informal, worded from the couple themselves. Here are just a couple of examples:

Mr S Craig and Miss R Smith
The engagement is announced between Stuart, eldest son of Mr and Mrs Steven Craig of Godalming Surrey, and Rianne Smith, youngest daughter of Mr and Mrs Charles Smith of Harrogate, Yorks.

Stuart Craig and Rianne Smith
Stuart Craig, the eldest son of Mr and Mrs Steven Craig of Godalming, Surrey, and Rianne Smith, youngest daughter of Mr and Mrs Charles Smith of Harrogate, Yorks, are delighted to announce their recent engagement.

Today you're likely to tell close family face-to-face or by phone and let the rest of the world know via email or a social networking site. The only people who officially announce their engagements in public these days are royalty via a 'Buckingham Palace Spokesman' and popular 'royalty' like soap stars and footballers who do it from the pages of celebrity glossies for large amounts of cash.

 SHOULD WE THROW AN ENGAGEMENT PARTY?

It's very tempting to pop a few champagne corks and gather the troops for a celebration party, but engagement parties are not as popular as they were 20 years ago, when invited guests often turned up with engagement presents. Now a lot of couples see engagement parties as an unnecessary expense and a potential minefield over invitations.

There are pros and cons to having an engagement party. Here are just a few:

The pros:

- A party is a great way to spread the good news about the impending wedding.

- It can be a mini dry-run for the main event if you're not used to arranging parties, hiring venues or booking caterers.

- People might bring you presents.

- It's fun!

The cons:

- People invited to an engagement party often assume they are automatically coming to the wedding, too.

- You may feel guilty that the money could be better spent on the wedding.

- Friends will be lobbying to see if they are on the list for best man/chief bridesmaid and you may be compromised into asking too many people (or the wrong people) to be attendants.

Pocket fact ✿

At their engagement party in a country hotel in Nantwich, Victoria and David Beckham ordered an engagement cake to mark the occasion, but instead of cutting it in front of friends and family, they donated it to a fundraising event for a local primary school.

If you do decide to have an engagement party remember it doesn't have to be an elaborate affair. People will be happy about your good news and won't mind a small gathering at your local pub if that's the sort of thing you usually do.

✿ TIME FRAMES – HOW LONG TO ✿ BE ENGAGED?

There is no set length of time for an engagement – the trend in the UK now suggests couples are engaged for as long as two years but only actively plan their wedding for around a year. A long engagement is becoming increasingly popular with couples who want to fund or part-fund the celebrations themselves so that they can save up for the big day. It also means you are more likely to secure popular venues and suppliers on busy dates.

Pocket fact ✿

There are long engagements and there are long engagements. One Mexican couple, Octavio and Adriana, were engaged for a staggering 67 years before they finally got married in 1969 in their 80s.

However, there are those that say that a long engagement can be frustrating as the planning can take over your life, and you may even end up spending more as you give yourself time to consider every option available.

Pocket fact ✑

The average length of a marriage in modern Britain is 11 years, which is not a patch on Frank and Anita Milford who are thought to have enjoyed the longest marriage in Britain since the turn of the 20th century. The centenarians met at a YMCA dance and were married in May 1928. Eighty-one years later, in May 2009, they put their longevity down to: 'a little argument every day'. Sadly Frank died in September 2009, meaning they didn't equal what is thought to be the longest match in Britain — Thomas and Elizabeth Morgan of Caerleon in Wales who were married three months longer than the Milfords from May 1809 to January 1891.

🌺 THE LEGAL BIT 🌺

There are very few 'musts' in a modern wedding, formal etiquette and traditions which couples previously followed to the letter have gone out of fashion, but there are a few legal rules that apply to everyone. Although it may seem a bit unromantic there are some legal requirements you have to adhere to before you can tie the knot.

A LEGALLY BINDING ENGAGEMENT

A modern engagement has no legal standing in modern Britain, unlike 150 years ago. Back in the era of chaperones and stiff collars, a hopeful groom would nervously ask the stern Victorian father for his daughter's hand in marriage. Once he had that permission, he would then propose formally, on one knee, to the young lady in question. And when that was all done the young suitor was legally obliged to follow through on his betrothal. If he tried backing out on the deal, he was considered a cad and a scoundrel and his erstwhile fiancée and her family could chase him in the courts for breach of promise.

Nowadays though there are no legal obligations surrounding an engagement, apart from the tricky question of what to do with the ring if things don't work out.

THE BASIC LEGAL REQUIREMENTS OF GETTING MARRIED

There are very few 'musts' in a modern wedding. Lots of formal etiquette and traditions which couples previously followed to the letter have gone out of fashion, but there are a few legal rules that apply to everyone:

- Both of you must be free to marry of your own consent (divorcees must have a decree absolute) and not be close blood relatives. There are even restrictions on certain relationships between in-laws and adoptive families (see below), so if there is any doubt, check with your wedding official.

- If you are 16 or 17 years of age you cannot marry without parental consent. Each parent with parental responsibility can give parental consent.

- The wedding party must comprise a minimum of five people: the official, the bride and groom (one born female and one born male) and two adult witnesses.

- You must give notice of your intention to marry, either via an entry into the marriage book at your register office (for civil and non-Anglican weddings) or via the publication of marriage banns for a Church of England ceremony.

- You must marry in a recognised place of worship or in premises licensed for civil ceremonies – a register office or approved venues such as a hotel or stately home. Scottish law allows more flexibility, including weddings at home, because in Scotland it is the celebrant, rather than the venue, which is licensed.

- Weddings must be conducted between the hours of 8am and 6pm (with the exception of Jewish weddings where evening ceremonies are permitted).

Pocket fact &

For a modern religious ceremony, the banns announcing your coming marriage need to be read in the bride and groom's parish church on three consecutive Sundays. Today it's called reading the banns, in the 16th century it was known as crying the banns.

Who you CAN'T marry

The laws of consanguinity (which literally means connected by blood, from sang, the French word for blood) dictate that no one can legally marry a blood relative. This includes:

- *Mother*
- *Father*
- *Daughter*
- *Son*
- *Grandmother*
- *Grandfather*
- *Granddaughter*
- *Grandson*

- *Sister*
- *Brother*
- *Aunt*
- *Uncle*
- *Niece*
- *Nephew*
- *Grandparents*
- *Grandchildren*

Outside of blood ties, there are also laws against marrying certain people in your adoptive family. For instance, you can't marry your adoptive dad, but you could marry your adopted brother. There are also restrictions covering marriages to step-relatives and certain in-laws, so if there is any doubt whatsoever, get legal advice from a family solicitor or from the Citizens Advice Bureau.

Pocket fact &

The volume of marriages peaked in the late 60s and early 70s as the post-war baby boomers grew up, fell in love and said 'I do', but numbers have gradually declined since.

PLANNING TIMELINE

At this point you might feel a bit overwhelmed at the thought of all the planning you have to do. Don't panic, planning your wedding is supposed to be fun. This timeline is a rough guide to help you figure out what to plan when and help you keep on top of everything you need to do.

No two weddings are going to be exactly the same but there are a few logical steps to take at certain times to make sure everything is ready for the big day.

Remember, this is supposed to be fun. You're preparing for the biggest, most exciting day of your life. It's not an exam or a job interview and you are not being marked. You cannot 'fail' at planning a wedding. Your biggest challenge at this stage is to follow your own instincts and try not to let other people with their own agenda start running the show. So big smile, deep breaths and . . . enjoy!

Popular themes for weddings

Village fete — *bunting hung around an open-sided marquee or gazebo; vintage-style jugs and tea cups containing wild flowers; tiers of cupcakes with coconut ice and chocolate brownies; apple bobbing, guess-how-many-sweets-in-the-jar and other sideshows.*

Beside the sea — *navy and mid-blue tablecloths and napkins tied with raffia; tables named after seaside resorts or famous ships or mariners; shells to decorate the tables; mini fish and chips served in cones of newspaper; vases of coloured sand; an ice-cream van.*

Winter wonderland — *white roses and gerberas with mistletoe, ivy, holly and hypericum berries; large glass containers of gold and silver baubles; fairy lights draped around containers of willow; mulled wine and mince pies and, of course, a Christmas tree.*

Kasbah — *Bedouin-style tents with richly-coloured cushion seating; scented candles of musk and cinnamon; potted palms and Moroccan lanterns; meze buffet including hummus, baba ganoush (aubergine dip) and tagines; a belly dancer, obviously, although we wouldn't recommend a snake charmer!*

Hollywood — *clapperboards as centre pieces with tables named after screen icons; a band playing movie themes or record your own on CD; thank-you gifts presented like Oscars during the speeches; movies such as* It's a Wonderful Life *or* Father of the Bride *projected onto a big screen or white wall.*

Period drama — *readings from Jane Austen; an Empire line gown accessorised with a Georgian-style riding jacket; embroidered waistcoat and large cravat; feathered fans for the bridesmaids; string quartet playing 18th century country dances; British classics like chestnut soup, venison and syllabub.*

Eco-friendly — *recycled paper for the invitations and wedding stationery; dried leaves inscribed with names for place settings; one mode of transport to ferry guests around and save on car-miles; borrowed accessories; donations to charity gift lists in place of presents.*

Rock and roll — *invitations in the style of the old vinyl 45 records; grooms party and ushers dressed as Teddy Boys; a juke box for the musical entertainment; Elvis tribute act; a knee-length wedding gown in any colour but white.*

12 MONTHS BEFORE / AS EARLY AS POSSIBLE

- Agree a date, style (religious or civil) and a location for the wedding (which will depend on the style you've chosen). You might also want to think about whether you want a theme for your wedding.

- Set yourself a budget and discuss family contributions. If one or both sets of parents are going to help with the finances, it's best to get it out in the open early on.

- Consider hiring a wedding organiser. If you're going to hire professional help, get it from the start of your planning, not half way through when you've already got in a muddle.

- Start looking at ceremony and reception venues and ask them to pencil in your dates, if they are available, until you know you have both free on the same date. Most venues should hold it for you for a couple of weeks and you can ask them to contact you straight away if another couple is interested in the same date.

- Check all your friends and family members are free for your final date.

Stress buster

Now is the time to fine tune the art of delegation. Draw up a list of things you really want to handle yourselves — that includes all major decisions, obviously — then draw up a list that people can help with. Finding venues, menus, readings, accessories and decorations can be time consuming, so give trusted friends who want to help something to research.

- Book the church/ceremony venue and reception venue and pay deposits to secure dates. For a civil ceremony, make sure the district Superintendent Registrar is also free.

- Start shortlisting your florist, photographer, caterers and cake maker, especially if you have chosen a Saturday in high season. If you want a marquee, start talking to providers now.

- Take out wedding insurance as soon as you start paying deposits. It's a small amount for a lot of peace of mind. See pages 54–55 for more on wedding insurance.

- Draw up a rough guest list to work out the sort of numbers you're dealing with but don't make it public at this stage as things almost always change.

Pocket fact ✿

Save-the-date cards are becoming increasingly popular as a way to ensure your friends and family members are free for your big day. These can be sent out well in advance of the invitations, allowing people to plan travel arrangements etc. Save-the-date cards can also take more unusual or adventurous forms than invitations, such as postcards, fridge magnets, emails or even Valentine's Day cards.

NINE MONTHS BEFORE

- Pick your best man, chief bridesmaid, flower girls and ushers, particularly the first two as you're going to need all the help you can get in the run-up to the wedding, not just on the day.

- The longer you take to decide on your principal players the more of the organising you'll need to take on yourself.

- Make an appointment with your wedding official to discuss the content of your wedding and to book future appointments to choose music and readings. Some religious officials like you to attend pre-wedding 'classes' – usually quite informal evenings but they will need to go in the diary too.

- Start looking at honeymoon brochures. If you're going for the big holiday-of-a-lifetime trip you'll need to save.

- Start looking around for your dream gown, especially if you want a designer dress that will involve a number of fittings.

Pocket tip ♫

A big part of planning your wedding can be choosing who you want to be the chief bridesmaid or best man. While some people stick with tradition and ask brothers or sisters, others ask trusted friends. Either way make sure you consider whether they're the right choices to help you in all your organisation dramas and to perform their role on the big day.

SIX MONTHS BEFORE

- Start planning your bridesmaids' outfits, especially if they don't all live in the same part of the country and you need to get them together for fittings.

- If you haven't already booked them, make sure you have confirmed and paid deposits for suppliers such as DJ, entertainer, and wedding cars.

- Start looking for styles of wedding stationery you like. Although some of the final details like the menu and guest list won't be finalised until much nearer the time, get a good idea of when the deadlines for printing and proofs will be.

THREE TO SIX MONTHS BEFORE

- Order your rings, especially if you want them to be engraved.

- Book your honeymoon and make sure you have enough validity left on your passport. Lots of countries insist on six months.

- Arrange another meeting with your florist and photographer to finalise details including shot lists and ask them to come on a site visit to the venue with you if they have time.

- Book some food and wine tastings in plenty of time especially if you want printed menus.

- Make sure the groom's party have booked their outfit hire and all the necessary sizes are available.

- Finalise bridesmaids' outfits, taking into account the amount a child may grow in three months. Ask around for the name of a good dressmaker for any last-minute alterations.

- Book your hairstylist for a practice run of styling your hair with the veil or tiara.

- Book your make-up artist on the day if you're having one and start preparing your skin with some pampering facials

- Confirm music and service details with your minister or registrar in time for any orders of service to be ordered.

- Finalise the guests list, as invitations will have to go out soon.

Pocket tip 🔔

If you like the idea of booking your honeymoon under your married name you will need to make sure you update your passport to reflect this. Most airlines won't let you travel if your booking doesn't match your passport so give yourself plenty of time to get this sorted. See page 160 for more information.

TWO MONTHS BEFORE

- Invitations are usually sent 6–8 weeks in advance of the wedding so put together any useful inserts such as maps and nearby B&Bs which can be included. For summer weddings accommodation info is useful some weeks ahead of the invitation.

- Tick off all the accessories you're going to need – veil, shoes, underwear, jewellery – and look for some new swimwear for your honeymoon.

ONE MONTH BEFORE

- Ring all suppliers and double check delivery times and details. Pay any outstanding amounts.

- Chase guests who haven't sent back their RSVPs.

- As the RSVPs come in start working on a seating plan.

- Put together a playlist for the band or DJ, things you hate as well as things you love.

- Have your final dress fitting.

TWO WEEKS BEFORE

- Try on your whole outfit together in case you need a dress adjustment or extra jewellery.

- Finalise the numbers and menu with your venue, including special dietary needs.

- Arrange your hen/stag parties this week, so that you can recover!

ONE WEEK BEFORE

- Remind everyone about the ceremony rehearsal and go through all the final details such as who will need a lift, where the ushers will stand, where your overnight bag will be, who will carry your make-up etc.

- Send a final seating plan to the venue (with guests' names clearly spelled) and any place settings if you are writing them out yourself.

THE DAY BEFORE

- Go for a long walk, a swim, a sauna or a massage. You're in the final straight now and it's more about how you feel than what you can do at this stage.

- Have your nails done, wrap any thank-you gifts for brides-maids, and try to get a good night's sleep.

This checklist is by no means exhaustive but should guide you through the main points. Keep your own planning checklist or spreadsheet and make sure you update it regularly.

Pocket fact &

Marriage could be good for your health. Research shows that being married can add an extra three years on to a man's lifespan compared to his single counterpart. One theory is that security and mental stimulation psychologically promote wellbeing – another that women are just rather good at looking after their menfolk.

❧ EARLY DECISIONS ❧

At this early stage it's important to remember this is your day so you need to decide the kind of wedding you want to have and how to stamp your personality on the big day. Think about the things that really matter to you – the where, the when, the who, the how – and focus on these; the small details can be taken care of later.

Friends and family can often get carried away with all the excitement of a new engagement and bombard you with ideas of how they think you should do things. This is where all your skills of diplomacy come in to play. Dad may want you to book the local golf club, mum may have her eye on the fancy hotel in town and you may be thinking about keeping it simple and booking two flights to Vegas. However left-field their ideas may be, give the impression that you are considering all options and you're grateful for their input. Losing your rag with phrases like "you must be joking. . ." and "I wouldn't be seen dead in that place. . ." are not going to get proceedings off on the right foot!

Pocket tip 🎀

Wedding shows can be useful when you first get engaged. National shows in big cities bring hundreds of wedding suppliers under one roof and if you can get to them easily, they are worth the price of the ticket to get a good overview of the market. Smaller, local wedding fairs obviously focus more on suppliers in one area, so they can be helpful once you have settled on a location.

The first decision you need to make is the date. Once you have that sorted you can really get going. There's more on choosing the date on pages 33–37 but the main things you have to consider are the season, the availability of your venue and your guests and whether you want a custom made dress.

Once you've chosen a date for the big day, the number of venues you need to book will depend on your style of ceremony. Here's a quick rundown of the different types of ceremony you can have and what they will mean for your planning.

RELIGIOUS OR CIVIL?

Around 40% of couples in the UK now choose a religious ceremony, which almost always means two venues – the church, tem-
ple or other place of worship and then a reception location.

Pocket fact 🐚

*The earliest records for weddings being an official sacrament
within the church didn't start appearing until the 12th century.*

A civil ceremony in a register office will also need venue number
two for the celebration, but for the estimated 50% of couples that
choose a civil ceremony in a venue licensed as an approved premises, you can usually have your vows and your vino all in the same
place. There's no option for a wedding at home in England and
Wales as a venue (ie your home) cannot just be licensed for your
wedding – it must be available to any other couple who want to
marry there. This is why Prince Charles and Camilla couldn't get
married in Windsor Castle – the queen would have had to open
the portcullis to anyone else who fancied tying the knot there too.

Pocket tip 🔔

*Licensed venues in England and Wales must be permanent struc-
tures with a roof and a proper address, which means ceremonies
in the forest or on the beach are not legal. In Scotland it is the
official – the minister or registrar – not the location which is
licensed, so couples can marry beside a loch or half way up a
mountain if the official agrees.*

RELIGIOUS CEREMONIES

Many people like to stick with tradition and get married in a
church. Depending on your religion, or the type of church you
want to be married in, there are a few rules you need to follow
before you can say 'I do'.

If you're marrying in the Church of England, Church of Wales or the Scottish Episcopal Church, the minister is legally allowed to perform the civil part of the ceremony and act as registrar. In other denominations, this may also be possible but, again, assume nothing and consult with your minister of religion. For instance, in the Roman Catholic, Jewish and Quaker faiths ministers are usually authorised to register the marriage, as are most Greek Orthodox priests, but other faiths or denominations may require either a registrar or a civil ceremony before the religious ceremony to make the marriage legal.

Church of England and Church in Wales

Banns will be read on three consecutive Sundays in the weeks leading up to your wedding but no earlier than three months. If you live in different parishes or are on the electoral roll at a different parish, the banns will be read at both.

Church of Scotland

Unlike England and Wales, marriages can take place practically anywhere if the minister agrees and the location has a proper address, although you must also give notice to the registrar of the district in which you want to marry. Marriage of divorcees is more widely accepted than in England and Wales.

Roman Catholic

You need to register your intention to marry, as with a civil ceremony, and gain the marriage licence yourself. If you are both Catholic, the priest will ask to see either a baptism or confirmation certificate. If one of you is not a Catholic, you will need a 'dispensation' usually from the priest or a bishop. Make sure you approach your chosen church at least six months before the date you have chosen.

Jewish

As with all non-Anglican faiths, legal applications must be made to local register offices as in a civil ceremony, although most rabbis are authorised to register the marriage on the day. Jewish law bans weddings on the Sabbath, although they are exempt from the law stating that wedding must take place before 6pm meaning evening ceremonies are popular. Jewish weddings do not have to be held in a place of worship but can be at secular locations such as a hotel under the traditional canopy called a *chuppah*.

Wider choice of church

As the numbers of couples choosing religious ceremonies continued to fall in the UK, the Church of England decided to take action. Rather than restricting couples to their local parish church, in 2008 the Church of England Marriage Measure gave couples a wider choice providing they could prove a connection with their chosen church. The seven reasons you can use for applying for a church wedding outside your local parish are:

1. One of you has lived in the parish for at least six months
2. One of you was baptised in the parish
3. One of you was prepared for confirmation in the parish
4. One of you has regularly gone to normal church services in the parish for at least six months
5. One of you has a parent/parents who lived in the parish for six months at any time after you were born
6. One of you has a parent/parents who has regularly gone to normal services in the parish church for at least six months
7. One of you has parents or grandparents that were married in the parish

Pocket fact ✇

Humanist ceremonies often suit couples who want a spiritual but non-denominational ceremony. Although humanist weddings are legal in Scotland, they are not legally recognised in England and Wales so you would have to have a quick civil ceremony at a register office first. But the flexibility of a Humanist ceremony means you can exchange vows outdoors, at home or on a moving boat, providing you can find a celebrant to agree. Couples who choose a humanist ceremony often write their own vows and celebrants are usually happy to help with this. Details at www.humanist.org.uk.

 TEN MOVIES TO GET YOU IN THE MOOD

Weddings, it seems, are big box office. Hardly a year goes by without one of the big studios releasing a film on a wedding theme. Some are awful, most are amusing and a few are absolute classics. Here are 10 of the best.

1. Father of the Bride

1950, starring Spencer Tracy and Elizabeth Taylor

Story in a nutshell: Tracy plays a curmudgeonly lawyer who discovers his long-lost sentimental gene after the whirlwind wedding plans for daughter Kay, played by Taylor. Comic themes include Tracy muttering about the greed of the wedding industry and the fact that the role of the bride's father is to do little more than sign cheques and keep quiet.

Reasons to watch: The script and pace are touching, gentle and life-affirming and the performance from Tracy is exceptional. It may be 60 years old, but the worries and niggles are universal. One to watch with dad.

Classic line: *'An experienced caterer can make you ashamed of your house in 15 minutes'*

2. Four Weddings and a Funeral

1994, starring Hugh Grant and Andie MacDowell

Story in a nutshell: Serial wedding guest Charles (Grant) seems destined to stay single forever, until he is captivated by an enigmatic American (MacDowell). A succession of different weddings looks at the nature of friendship from the viewpoint of the guests for once rather than the couple.

Reasons to watch: For its wonderful snapshot of British wedding clichés from the dreary receiving line to the sex-starved bridesmaid, and the fact that, apart from the funeral storyline, most characters meet their life mates in a feel-good ending. One to watch while you're wrestling with your guest list.

Classic line: 'Why do they call it a honeymoon?' *'I suppose it's "honey" cos it's as sweet as honey and "moon" because it was the first time a husband got to see his wife's bottom.'*

3. Father of the Bride

1992, starring Steve Martin and Diane Keaton

Story in a nutshell: A slapstick remake of the 1950 Spencer Tracy film with George Banks (Martin) doing everything in his power to cut the excesses of his daughter's wedding, in the face of mighty opposition – namely wife Nina (Keaton) and eccentric, but totally indecipherable, wedding planner Frank, pronounced Fraaank, played by Martin Short.

Reasons to watch: Accutely funny observational comedy about curbing guest lists and trying to trim a budget that's spiralling out of control. One to watch with mum.

Classic line: *'I used to think a wedding was a simple affair. Boy and girl meet, he buys a ring, she buys a dress, they said "I do". I was wrong. That's getting married. A wedding is entirely different.'*

4. My Best Friend's Wedding

1997, starring Julia Roberts, Cameron Diaz and Rupert Everett

Story in a nutshell: Former lovers Julianne (Roberts) and Michael (Dermot Mulroney) once made a pledge that if neither is married by the age of 28, they would marry each other. When Michael announces his engagement to Kimberley (Diaz), Julianne decides she wants Michael back and does everything in her power to scupper the wedding.

Reasons to watch: For Cameron Diaz's ear-shattering karaoke rendition of *I just don't know what to do with myself*, Rupert Everett's hilarious turn as Julianne's gay best friend George and the classic scene when everyone at the rehearsal dinner breaks into an ensemble performance of *I say a little prayer*. One to watch if your other half is muttering about inviting an ex!

Classic line: *'Maybe there won't be marriage, maybe there won't be sex, but by God there'll be dancing'*

5. My Big Fat Greek Wedding

2002, starring Nia Vardalos and John Corbett

Story in a nutshell: Greek-American Toula (Vardalos) falls for Ian (Corbett) but her father is not impressed that she is marrying a non-Greek boy and makes no bones about it.

Reasons to watch: For the fairytale ugly duckling parody – except that frumpy waitress Toula was never really ugly, just lacking in confidence and overwhelmed by her larger-than-life family. Also great for gentle comic observations rather than slapstick. One to watch with anyone in your family who's being a pain!

Classic line: *'Nice Greek girls are supposed to do three things in life; marry Greek boys, make Greek babies and feed everyone till the day we die.'*

6. The Wedding Singer

1998, starring Adam Sandler and Drew Barrymore

Story in a nutshell: Adam Sandler plays a wedding singer, Robbie, who has no luck in his own marriage stakes when he is jilted at the altar. He is rescued emotionally by waitress Julia (Barrymore) and roped into helping with her wedding arrangements, eventually meaning Julia realises that she is marrying a man who takes her for granted and she is in fact in love with Robbie.

Reasons to watch: For its fabulous pastiche of 1980s fashion and music, plus great lead performances from Sandler and Barrymore as losers in love who find happiness. One to watch with your other half – it never does to get complacent.

Classic line: *'I wanna make you smile whenever you're sad, Carry you around when your arthritis is bad, All I wanna do is grow old with you.'*

7. Arthur

1981, starring Dudley Moore, John Gielgud and Liza Minnelli

Story in a nutshell: Arthur (Moore) is a drunken millionaire being forced into a marriage with an heiress, Susan, when he falls for down-at-the-heel waitress Linda (Minnelli) instead. When his family threaten to cut him off without a penny he is torn between his playboy lifestyle and his heart.

Reasons to watch: Dab a tear at the tender scenes when frosty butler Hobson (Gielgud) melts just enough to help the course of true love on its way and roar with laughter at Moore's drunken arrival at his own wedding as he tries to wriggle out of going through with the ceremony. One to watch when you're struggling with your wedding budget – true love conquers all!

Classic line: Susan: *'Arthur, will you take my hand?'* Arthur: *'That would leave you with one.'*

8. The Wedding Planner

2001, starring Jennifer Lopez and Matthew McConaughey

Story in a nutshell: Wedding planner Mary (Lopez) is unlucky in love herself but loses herself in her work planning upmarket weddings, until she meets a handsome doctor Steve (McConaughey) during a traffic incident and falls for his charms. Unfortunately he is the groom for the wedding she is planning!

Reasons to watch: To snigger at the opulence and over-the-top extravagance of the weddings Mary plans with military precision and to recognise how so much of it is fluff. One to watch with your bridesmaids on a girly night in.

Classic line: *'Y'know those who can't, teach? Well, those who can't wed, plan.'*

9. Guess Who's Coming to Dinner

1967, starring Sidney Poitier, Spencer Tracy and Katherine Hepburn

Story in a nutshell: Tracy and Hepburn play waspish Matt and Christina faced with the sudden news that their daughter is engaged to be married to John, a black doctor. Matt struggles with the social attitudes of the day, as do John's parents who are invited to dinner, until all four come to acknowledge that love is colour blind.

Reasons to watch: The interaction between the two young lovers is secondary to the fantastic dialogue between Hepburn and Tracy, caught between oppressive social mores and family loyalty. One to watch with gran who'll tell you just what an impact the film made when it first came out.

Classic line: *'You're two wonderful people who happen to fall in love and happen to have a pigmentation problem.'*

10. Muriel's Wedding

1995, starring Toni Colette and Rachel Griffiths

Story in a nutshell: Muriel (Colette) is a gauche and frumpy small town girl in Australian backwater Porpoise Spit, dreaming of ABBA and marriage, until she gets her hands on some money and runs off to follow her dream. She haunts wedding shops and does eventually get married, to the wrong man, before realising that before she finds Mr Right, she has to find herself.

Reasons to watch: For its laughs but also for its tender and sad moments and for understanding that weddings are more than big day set pieces. One to watch with your bridesmaids.

Classic line: On the throwing of the bouquet *'What's the use of you having it Muriel. No one's ever gonna marry you. You've never even had a boyfriend. Cheryl's been going with Shane for over six weeks. She's next.'*

3

THE BIG DECISIONS

🌿 SETTING THE DATE 🌿

Although May to September was traditionally high season for weddings in the UK, couples are making much more use of the rest of the year now, and autumn and winter celebrations are definitely on the up. Venues are also very keen to welcome big parties through their doors midweek and in the depths of November or February, so you can often negotiate yourselves a better deal than if you wanted to celebrate on a Saturday in the summer.

WHICH SEASON IS BEST?

Spring: March – May

Pros: It's the beginning of the traditional 'wedding season' and many public and historic venues will have been closed for spring cleaning, so will be looking their best. Trees will be blossoming and colourful and a good sunny spring day looks fresh in the photos. The clocks don't go forward until the end of March, so choose an early-ish ceremony if you want natural sunlight in your photos.

Cons: There isn't much to say against a spring wedding, other than you have a 50/50 chance of rain in early spring as March averages 14–15 days rain per year. Weddings close to Easter may push up venue and flower prices and there are often restrictions on church weddings during Lent.

Summer: June – August

Pros: July and August record the highest temperatures of the year so now is the time to have that country fete-themed wedding, marquee, or barbecue. You have the best chance of making the most of beautiful gardens and grounds at your venue.

Cons: Family and friends with children may be limited to going on holiday outside term time so for weddings at the end of July and throughout August you might need to warn people a long way in advance with save-the-date cards. Your wedding could also clash with others and people may find themselves double-booked, especially on Saturdays, so why not consider a Friday or a Sunday wedding? Venues and good suppliers are booked up a long way in advance – often up to two years – another reason to think beyond Saturday weddings.

Pocket tip 🔔

The eastern side of Britain tends to be slightly drier than the west BUT when it does rain during the summer, the rain is heavier than it would be in the winter!

Autumn: September – November

Pros: The clocks don't usually go back until the end of October so early autumn is a brilliant time for romantic low lighting, especially in the late afternoon, early evening. Burnished golds and russets on the trees are a great inspiration for colour themes, along with harvest festival, Halloween and bonfire night.

Cons: October is an infamously windy month and there will be more of a chill in the air. The days will be growing shorter so there are fewer hours for photography.

Winter: December – February

Pros: After the Christmas rush, venues and suppliers are keen to encourage weddings in January and February and could be very amenable to some haggling and discounting. A candlelit winter wedding is a great theme, or you can have a Christmas theme, complete with tree and carols. January can be a flat month with not many invitations flying around so guests may be keen to dress up and come out to join you. You won't be disappointed with the weather – it's going to be cold – but you could be pleasantly surprised if you get a crisp bright winter's day.

Cons: Before Christmas, venues can be very busy, your guests could be caught up with other events. Some churches don't have the availability for your dream Christmas wedding, or impose restrictions. People don't have a lot of money spare around Christmas and New Year, especially for things like hen weekends or overnight accommodation at the wedding itself.

Saturday is not the only day

For years Saturday has been the traditional day to get married (apart from couples in the Jewish faith as Saturday is the Sabbath and couples are not permitted to marry on the Sabbath) but a growing trend is emerging for weekday weddings. Friday is the second most popular day, followed by Sunday. Midweek is less popular, as it often means guests have to take two days off work, but it does give you great bargaining power with venues and suppliers. For a Saturday wedding, you may have to wait up to two years for a great venue or a top photographer; with a mid-week wedding, you have the negotiating power and may be able to secure a discount or a better wedding package for your money.

Pocket fact ✿

29 September is Michaelmas, traditionally when the good wives of medieval Scotland traditionally dug up carrots in the hope that any earth pulled up with the vegetables would bring them fertility. So if you don't like rich fruit cake, use this custom as an excuse to have carrot cake instead and decorate with Michaelmas daisies (also known as asters).

DATES TO AVOID

Go through your diary/address book and check dates like family birthdays or significant anniversaries that might be coming up in the next year. If your aunt and uncle's silver wedding anniversary or your nephew's 18th birthday falls on the weekend you're considering for your wedding, you may have a conflict of interests. This is where it can be useful to send out save-the-date cards, even if you haven't firmed up a venue yet. Also check that there are no disruptive sporting events in the area on the dates you have pencilled in. A big race meeting or sporting final can play havoc with the traffic and availability of hotel accommodation in the area. It might also make sense to make sure there are no cup final or World Cup qualifier games on that day as well: you don't want your groom leaving every 20 minutes to check the score!

Pocket tip

Bank holidays are a bit of a two-edged sword when it comes to weddings. They are good from the guests' point of view because it means they can make a mini break out of your celebrations without using up a day's annual leave. On the downside, venues and suppliers often put up their rates because they know demand will outstrip supply.

Lucky (and not so lucky) months

This traditional rhyme is thought to date back to the Middle Ages:
   'Married when the year is new, he'll be loving, kind and true.
   When February birds do mate, you neither wed nor dread
      your fate.
   If you wed when March winds blow, joy and sorrow both
      you'll know.
   Marry in April when you can, Joy for Maiden and for Man.
   Marry in the month of May, and you'll surely rue the day.
   Marry when June roses grow, over land and sea you'll go.
   Those who in July do wed must labour for their daily bread.
   Whoever wed in August be, many a change is sure to see.
   Marry in September's shrine, your living will be rich and fine.
   If in October you do marry, love will come but riches tarry.
   If you wed in bleak November, only joys will come, remember.
   When December snows fall fast, marry and true love will last.'

Pocket fact ❧

The most popular wedding date in 2009 was 12 September and it's not the first time the second weekend of September has seen a frenzy of wedding activity. On 11 September 2005, no less than five high-profile couples got married. Katie Price and Peter Andre; model Jodie Kidd and Aidan Butler; Sara Buys and Tom Parker Bowles; GMTV's Kate Garraway and Derek Draper; and Coronation Street's Samia Ghadie and Matthew Smith (although the first two couples have since gone their separate ways!).

✿ SETTING YOUR BUDGET ✿

According to the annual Cost of a Wedding survey conducted by *You & Your Wedding* magazine in 2009, the average cost of a wedding is £19,265. There are stories about brides (especially in the commercially adroit US) who have recouped some of the cost of their wedding by letting local companies leave their business cards on the tables for guests to pick up! Others have had their weddings sponsored by local industry in return for logos on the stationery and mentions in the speeches. If you're thinking of keeping your wedding a slightly more intimate affair, a tight budget, a financial spreadsheet and a will of iron is going to be needed.

Try to agree a rough guest list early, as this will affect all your sliding costs (venue size, food, drink etc). Your own outfits, rings and church or licence fees are fixed costs which are unaffected by your numbers. Traditionally the bride's parents paid for most of the day, including the reception, while church fees, cars and honeymoon were often covered by the groom's side. Although this custom is still followed in some families, it is more usual for the couple to contribute to (or even pay for) their own wedding. Today, only 10% of couples expect the bride's family to foot the whole bill and nearly half of all couples use a contribution approach.

USEFUL QUESTIONS TO ASK YOUR SUPPLIERS

Q: Is that really the best price you can do?

Most suppliers will quote a little higher than they're prepared to accept – it's usual business practice – so if you take their first offer, they have a real result. Try to negotiate as most people are prepared to drop the price if you're prepared to haggle or make it a condition of your decision to book. Don't try haggling after you've agreed a price though!

Q: Does the price include VAT?

If not, you have to add on another 17.5% to most things! Nasty shocks all round.

Q: How much deposit do you want and when do we have to pay the balance?

If you have all the dates on a big wedding spreadsheet you can see the hard months coming with plenty of warning.

Pocket fact ✍

The biggest expense at a wedding is entertaining guests (venue hire, catering, drinks and entertaining), taking around 37% of the budget.

KEEPING TABS ON YOUR BUDGET

No wedding needs everything in this list, but it's a good guide for what you might need and how to keep track of what you've spent and what you still have to pay.

What for?	Deposit	Balance
Church fees	. . . . .	. . . . .
Choir/organist/bells (if extra)	. . . . .	. . . . .
Copyright fee (for a video)	. . . . .	. . . . .
Register office fees	. . . . .	. . . . .

Venue hire (ceremony)	. . . . .	. . . . .
Wedding insurance	. . . . .	. . . . .
Reception venue	. . . . .	. . . . .
Marquee	. . . . .	. . . . .
Drinks and canapés	. . . . .	. . . . .
Catering	. . . . .	. . . . .
Evening bar	. . . . .	. . . . .
Bar/waiting staff	. . . . .	. . . . .
Decorations	. . . . .	. . . . .
Wedding cake	. . . . .	. . . . .
Entertainment	. . . . .	. . . . .
DJ	. . . . .	. . . . .
Fireworks	. . . . .	. . . . .
Transport	. . . . .	. . . . .
Photographer	. . . . .	. . . . .
Videographer	. . . . .	. . . . .
Flowers	. . . . .	. . . . .
Bride's dress	. . . . .	. . . . .
Veil/headdress	. . . . .	. . . . .
Hair (incl. practice sessions)	. . . . .	. . . . .
Groom's outfit	. . . . .	. . . . .
Shoes and accessories	. . . . .	. . . . .
Bride's jewellery	. . . . .	. . . . .
Wedding rings	. . . . .	. . . . .
Attendants' outfits	. . . . .	. . . . .
Thank-you gifts	. . . . .	. . . . .

Pocket fact 💍

What with wedding gifts, outfits, hen/stag parties, travel and accommodation and drinks at the bar, wedding guests in Britain spend an average of £226 per person to see their friends and family say 'I do', with over 10% spending over £500. So it's not just you spending money!

THE GUEST LIST: CUTTING COSTS BY CUTTING NUMBERS

Guests – however much you love them – are a cost per head so you have to decide whether you're going to invite the number of guests to fit your venue or your budget. Just because your dream stately home can seat 200 in the ballroom, doesn't mean you have to make up the numbers to suit the space.

It may seem idyllic to share the most exciting day of your lives with everyone you've ever known, but your guest list is the one area where cost can quickly spiral out of control, so when you set your budget be realistic, logical and firm with parents/friends putting on pressure.

Ten ways to control your guest list

1. Draw up two lists of who you *need* to invite, who you'd *like* to invite. They don't have to be mutually exclusive but it will identify how many you're only considering because you feel you have to. Guilt invitations should not be your top priority – you want to be surrounded by people you love and who have earned their place at the celebration, not by people you feel you 'owe'.

2. Categorise your lists into close family, distant family, old friends (school, college, university), current friends (people you see all the time) and workmates. It helps to prioritise the numbers and helps you see how many potential tables you might need.

Pocket tip

Unless you have a limitless budget you probably can't ask every-one you know. If you have to get ruthless with which friends to invite and which to leave out, organise them in the way you would your wardrobe. If you haven't worn a coat in a year, it'll probably go on the 'no' pile. If you haven't seen a friend in a year, there's probably a good reason.

3. A guest list isn't territory to be divided equally between families so don't give both sets of parents the same number of guests they can invite. Ask instead who they would like in a non-committal sort of way and see how closely the figures match. You don't want one side inviting random distant cousins just to make up the numbers.

4. Decide if you're including children in the total. A lot of couples now restrict children to close family and friends only and ask other guests to leave their kids at home. But do this early on with a phone call or face-to-face, don't leave it till you send the invitations. (See Common Wedding Problems, page 167.)

5. Are workmates going to be included? If so, will they also get to bring a plus-one, especially if you don't know their partners well, if at all? People often don't mind coming alone but in a group, providing you tell them early enough before they assume the opposite.

Rule of thumb 🎂

Beware of inviting your manager because you feel you have to. What you do in your social life should have no bearing on your work relationships. Asking the boss to come could make you, him/her and other workmates feel awkward and could even smack of crawling. Unless you and the boss are friendly socially already – do you go out for lunch together or socialise after work? – it may be best to leave him or her out.

---

6. Tactfully resist quid pro quo invitations from parents who want to invite their friends – the old 'well, we went to their son's wedding . . .' argument. It might be a bit awkward for them, but that's not your responsibility.

7. Have an evening-only list but make it sound like a really exclusive party. If you can afford to print separate invitations, put something like *'Time to party! Please join us for*

cocktails and dancing at xxpm' and make sure you have welcome drinks standing by, along with yourselves, so that people don't feel like they are coming along at the tail end of the main event.

8. Check early on if relatives who live far away or even overseas are going to be able to make it. You don't want to find out six weeks before the wedding that the Canadian contingent was never going to make it.

9. If you have a reserve list for when you start getting RSVPs saying 'sorry, can't come', don't mention it to anyone. No one wants to feel second best. Instead, try to imply that you are able to invite someone last-minute because you have flexibility for more numbers, not because someone dropped out.

10. Be careful about discussing your hen/stag parties. If someone thinks they are invited to the stag or hen party they will almost certainly expect an invite to the wedding itself.

Pocket fact 🍸

There's nothing like a mass wedding to trim a budget and Valentine's Day is a popular date for plural promises. On 14 February 2006, 83 couples were married or renewed their vows at the Lakeland Ski resort in Colorado, USA, at a height of 12,400 feet. On the same date three years later (2009) a staggering 390 couples were married in Manila in the Philippines! But that's small potatoes to the Korean brides and grooms of the Unification Church at Sun Moon University. In October 2009 an estimated 5,000 couples joined in a mass celebration near Seoul.

CHOOSING THE VENUE

There's no point choosing a colour scheme or booking a DJ until you have a venue. After the date and the location, the address on your invitation is crucial. Whether you're looking for a ceremony and reception all in one, or a venue for your reception only, there are a few key questions to ask before you make a booking.

USEFUL QUESTIONS TO ASK THE VENUE

Q: Are we the only wedding party?

If you're likely to be on a conveyor belt of two, or even three events that day (depending on the size of the venue) make sure any other celebrations won't have any knock-on effects. Will the bars be rammed or will the car park be overflowing? Another small anniversary lunch might go unnoticed; another big wedding could cramp your style.

Q: Are there rooms available for guests at the venue or at hotels or B&Bs nearby?

How close is local transportation (station, airport, taxi) and parking facilities for guests who aren't staying the night?

Q: Is the venue an exclusive-live?

For example, do we have to book all (or a set number) of rooms to secure the booking and for how many nights?

Q: What happens if it rains?

Don't cross your fingers and hope for the best. Always have a plan B.

Q: What restrictions are there?

Know the rules before you sign on the dotted line. Some venues, especially historic and listed buildings don't allow tea lights or candles; a few even have a restriction on red wine because of the damage it can cause if it spills. Can you have fireworks and is there a time that the music has to be switched off?

Q: Can we use our own suppliers or do we have to use yours?

Some venues insist on supplying the food and drink and like to recommend the florist and DJ etc. Unless their suppliers are prohibitively expensive – or you have a florist in the family – it's usually a good idea to at least check out their nominations. On the plus side they will all be used to working together.

Q: Can we have access the day before?

If you are having elaborate floral arches or if friends are helping you to decorate, having access the day before is useful, because it means you can get involved in directing the decorations too.

Q: What exactly is included in my wedding package?

Venues are businesses and need to turn a profit, so be sure you know exactly what's included in the deal and what is extra. Things you might assume are included but could cost you include:

- A Facility room: will there be a room available for the bridal party to set ready or freshen up after the ceremony?

- Linen: if you're offered coloured tablecloths, napkins etc to go with your scheme, check they are not an additional cost. One hundred times anything soon mounts up.

- Chair backs: pretty but not vital. The chairs may look plain when you view the empty room at the venue, but they won't look so ordinary when the room is full of people in all their colourful finery.

- Cake stand and cake knife: this is often an extra cost even though you supply the cake! If it is extra, ask your cake maker if they could throw in the equipment as part of the price.

- After dinner coffee: some venues don't include this in the price per head and this is one of those little extras that soon creeps up.

- A room for people to change, nursing mums to take babies: many venues will make one available if they have one but don't take it for granted.

Pocket fact &

In 2009 the average UK wedding featured 101 guests, down slightly from 111 the previous year – a sign of the financial times perhaps?

MARQUEES – PROS AND CONS

If you're struggling to find a venue with the right capacity for your numbers, a marquee could be the answer. It's a great way to celebrate at a summer wedding, either in its own right, or as an extension to your dream venue (that's just a little too small) but it can be a lot of extra work. There are two basic styles of marquee for weddings – a traditional circus-style tent with central poles and guy ropes, or a clear span pavilion-style marquee which is built around a metal frame. Other popular styles include Indian Raj tents, Berber-style tents, tee-pees (styled around the original North American Indian tents) and yurts, traditional Mongolian tents.

Questions to ask a marquee supplier

Q: How long will it take to put up/take down?

Q: Can we have it open/closed at the side depending on the weather?

Q: Do we need any kind of official permission from the local authority?

Q: How will we arrange cooking/serving facilities and will we need an overspill tent?

Q: How will we bring in the power and will you liaise with the catering company over power supply?

Q: Do we need additional lighting, heating, flooring and how much will this cost?

Q: Can we bring in portable loos?

Pocket tip

Coconut or coir matting is a more economical way to put down a marquee floor but for uneven ground — and the perfect setting for dancing — wooden flooring is best.

DESTINATION WEDDINGS

Around 15% of couples in the UK now choose to marry abroad. Unless you have relatives or friends in your chosen country to help with the planning, the smart money says you hire in some extra help — either via a specialist tour operator that understands the legalities and the product you're buying, or via an experienced destination wedding planner. There are many stories flying around of couples arriving at their French chateau or Italian Palazzo without the relevant documentation and having to return home to a quick ceremony in the register office afterwards, because the legalities were not all in place and they could only have a symbolic blessing!

Pocket fact

Residency requirements vary widely. In Las Vegas you can get married virtually straight off the plane, yet in France you're expected to live there for 40 days before the wedding.

If you're marrying abroad, you'll need to look out some, or all, of these documents:

- 10 year passport (valid for at least six months)
- Birth certificates
- An adoption certificate (if adopted), decree nisi (if divorced), a death certificate and previous marriage certificate (if you're widowed)
- An affidavit signed by a solicitor stating no legal objection to the marriage

- Proof stamped and signed by a solicitor of any name changed by deed poll

- Some countries ask you for a Certificate of No Impediment, obtainable from the Register Office in your area. Check with the high commission or embassy of the country you have chosen.

- Parental consent if you're deemed underage in your chosen country

MARRYING ABROAD – THE PROS

- You can avoid all the exhausting family politics of who to invite, who to leave out and who's paying for what, especially if it's just the two of you jumping on a plane.

- You can often get more for your money and many exotic destinations offer free or reasonably priced wedding packages if you book a certain level of suite for your honeymoon.

- You can often do it in a much shorter timeframe than at home. To secure a popular venue in the UK can mean waiting one to two years. Apart from observing the legal residency requirements (which vary from country to country) and paperwork clearance, you can often book a destination wedding in a matter of weeks.

- You can rely on the weather!

Pocket fact &

15% of couples questioned by an NOP/Mintel poll said they thought disappearing overseas to a destination wedding would help them deal with the guest list dilemmas.

MARRYING ABROAD – THE CONS

- You can just as easily cause family wrangles by limiting your numbers and making family and friends feel 'left out'.

- You may not get all the fuss and fanfare you were hoping for. Package weddings can feel a bit 'conveyor belt', especially in big hotel complexes, so ask how many celebrations they will have on the same day as you because this may mean you will be sharing some of the services with others (ie photographer, videographer, catering and serving staff).

- It can feel a little lonely if you just go on your own, and there's no one close to party with afterwards. On the flip side if you're having your honeymoon in the same place you get married you may find family and friends hanging about!

Pocket fact 🕮

The most popular destinations for weddings abroad include Italy, Cyprus, Greece, the Caribbean, the USA, Mexico, Thailand, Mauritius and the Seychelles.

🌿 WEDDING STATIONERY 🌿

You may struggle with compiling your guest list for months and months before the big day but the final decision doesn't have to be made public until six to eight weeks before the wedding which is when the invitations are traditionally sent. However you do need to think about invitations – and all your other wedding stationery – at least four to six months before you need them in order to leave enough time for proofreading and delivery.

Money saver

Save-the-date cards are a fairly new trend which crossed the Atlantic from the States, and are simply a more formal way of doing what people have done for years – tell everyone the date as soon as it is set. It's a nice touch if you have the budget but a few phone calls, a round-robin email or an announcement on Twitter or a social media site should get the word out there quickly enough.

INVITATIONS

Unless you're planning to ask everyone via email, you will need some form of invitation. Engraved cards offer the most classic look but can be pricey; thermography offers a similiar look with a smoother finish for less of your budget and digital printing is the most value-for-money if you're more interested in sticking to your budget than creating a wow factor. Remember when choosing a font that however decorative it is it still needs to be easy to read – you don't want people ending up at the wrong venue because they read the address wrong!

Making your own invitations

If you have a creative streak, a great way of adding a personal stamp to your celebrations is by making your own invitations, or embellishing standard designs you've ordered through a stationer. You'll need to buy all the card, envelopes, calligraphy pens and decorative items (such as ribbon, stickers, stamps, glitter etc) individually, so this is not necessarily always a budget option, but what you will need to invest is your time. This is often a great girly get-together, so maybe you can rally the troops and get your bridesmaids to help in return for a couple of bottles of wine.

If you don't have the time or inclination to make invites from scratch, have simple cards printed through a stationer and then decorate them with a motif – butterflies, love birds or floral emblems – that you can use throughout your day. One roll of pretty wallpaper or a length of ribbon can go along way if you're only adding a small strip to each. Or why not design your own monogram, perhaps using your initials? Browse craft shops such as Hobbycraft or haberdashery sections of department stores for inspiration before you settle on a design. Remember, piece-work takes time so start buying your bits and bobs and looking for volunteers several weeks before the invitations have to go out.

A bespoke design featuring ribbons and crystals, a photograph, sketch or your own monogram is obviously going to cost more than an established design from a catalogue. The same goes for the weight of card and format (flat card, folded or gate-fold) you choose. Invitations can be ordered with matching pre-printed RSVP cards which are also useful if you're offering guests a choice of menu, but if you want to give guests travel directions, hotel contacts, menu options and gift list details without committing to the expense of lots of extra printing why not set up a wedding website? There are lots of template packages around if you're not a whizz at html where you can put all the information everyone needs to find.

If you're taking the bespoke angle, why not create a design that reflects your personalities or your day? When actress Emilia Fox and fellow thespian Jared Harris invited 150 guests to celebrate their marriage in a tiny Norman church, the sketch on the front of the invitation showed a long queue stretching to get into a little church.

Pocket tip

Guests travelling a long way will be using satellite navigation systems so make sure you include the full postcode for the ceremony and reception venue on your invitations. For small venues in the country it can also help to include directions with specific landmarks as some tiny venues can be hard to locate even with a sat nav guiding you.

Wording your invitations

Once upon a time, wedding invitations were very formal and almost always sent by the bride's parents. However, invitation wording has evolved, not least because more and more couples are hosting their own celebration in a more informal way.

Traditional wording along the lines of:

'*Mr & Mrs Charles Bainbridge request the pleasure of xxxxxx at the marriage of their daughter, Lydia Bainbridge, to Mr Steven Biggins, at xxxxxx.*'

is now often replaced by:

'*Lydia and Steven (surnames optional) would like to invite xxxxxx to help them celebrate their marriage on xxxxxx.*'

Choose whichever style suits you as a couple and the kind of wedding you're having.

If the invitations are being sent from divorced parents and a remarried mother has a new name the rule of thumb is to include her new married name with her first name, ie: '*Mr Charles Bainbridge and Mrs Patricia Knowles request the pleasure of xxxx at the marriage of their daughter Lydia. . .*'

Stress buster

One neat way around the whole remarried / new name dilemma is to word the invitation differently starting with the names of the guests you are asking, ie: 'Christopher and Elaine Mitchell are invited to celebrate the marriage of Lydia and Steve on xxxxxxxx.'

Pocket tip

Give your guests as much detail as possible. If you are marrying on a week day, spell it out to them by putting **Friday** *17th July on the invitation, as people automatically think: weddings 5 Saturdays. And if the reception is for a fixed length (ie only until 9pm), include this finishing time to help guests plan journeys and babysitters.*

ORDERS OF SERVICE

These are traditionally used for religious ceremonies to help guide guests through the procedure and to give the details of the readings (the name, the author and the person reading it) and the hymns. All this information means the order of service can soon turn into a booklet (the more paper and printing, the more the expense) so if you're on a budget, consider printing one sheet only with the basic details, including hymn numbers and the verses you will be singing, and ask ushers to give out hymn books at the same time (remembering to collect them up again at the end). When you're ordering orders of service (unlike invitations) remember you do need one per person.

Pocket tip 🔔

Your minister may ask to see a proof of the order of service and check your readings before you get it printed so make sure you factor in enough time in the schedule to allow for this.

MENUS

These look lovely at every place setting but in these cost-conscious times do you really need to get them printed? If you've offered guests a choice on the invitations beforehand they don't really need them – there should be no surprises other than some people forget what they ordered! If you are serving a set menu without options, consider printing it on a large sheet of card and display-ing it next to the table plan, so at least people know what they are expecting, or print out enough for one menu card per table on your home computer using a nice script font and stick this onto laminated card.

PLACE NAMES

You can have these printed but they are equally easy to write out yourself (make use of anyone in the family with an artistic hand) or to make yourselves.

Three alternative place settings you can make yourself

For couples who are more time rich and cash poor how about:

1 Collecting as many smooth pebbles as you can find and
   writing everyone's first name on them with a silver or
   gold art pen — great for a wedding by the sea.

2 Drying large fallen leaves and writing the names on them —
   great for a late autumn wedding.

3 Tying an old fashioned luggage label with the names written
   in bright red sparkly pen around a sprig of mistletoe — great
   for a Christmas wedding.

TABLE PLANS

This is worth the investment if the budget can stand it because
every guest will study this in detail to see where they are sitting in
relation to everyone else. Remember if you're going to have it
professionally printed, the company you use will need a definitive
list in advance, so you won't be able to do any last minute substi-
tutions the night before. Many venues also include a table plan in
the price of their wedding package, although this may be a simple
lists of names.

Pocket tip

*Forget the RSVP cards and ask people to email their reply, along
with a jpeg photo of a favourite shot of all of you — the photo
will make sure they don't forget to reply and you can make a fabulous slideshow of all the images which you could project onto a
screen or wall, or even show on a laptop, while people are queuing to join the receiving line.*

DO I NEED A WEDDING PLANNER?

In *The Wedding Planner* (2001) Jennifer Lopez feeds a
nervous groom his speech via an earpiece, saying to a startled
guest the immortal line, '*What? You think Kissinger came up with
his own stuff?*' Most planners will agree, this is an extreme
example although they are usually happy to help with most

aspects of wedding planning, aside from family politics and finding the groom!

Some charge a flat fee, while others will charge a percentage of the wedding budget but can usually save you the value of their fee by helping you negotiate with suppliers, sharing their money-saving expertise, and saving you unnecessary costs by securing discounts or bulk deals. When it comes to getting value for money, a professional knows where there are savings to be made in your catering or drinks bill, for instance, and in practical terms will know from experience how long certain parts of the day are likely to take. They will also save you time by undertaking negotiations and chasing up suppliers on your behalf. In effect, you can pay someone to have the stress for you! Many different packages are available, from a wedding co-ordinator who will work with you right from the beginning, sourcing an historic or unusual location, to someone who will look after the day-to-day running once you have made your key decisions.

Pocket tip

Some wedding planners offer an on-the-day-only service. This is obviously cheaper than the full planning package, but you're also hiring someone to do damage control when they've had no hand in organising the event. If you're worried about things going wrong on the day, pick a good best man!

DO I NEED WEDDING INSURANCE?

Most policies cover public liability insurance, which is often required when you are hiring stately homes (or if you have a marquee and don't want to be held responsible if someone trips on the ropes after one too many). Even if you've started your preparations, some policies will cover you retrospectively for deposits already paid before the policy was activated. They are also very useful if, heaven forbid, the day has to be cancelled due to ill-ness or bereavement, and will prevent you from losing all your deposits.

WHAT YOUR WEDDING INSURANCE MIGHT COVER (REMEMBER, POLICIES VARY SO READ THE SMALL PRINT!)

- **Cancellation** – if you have to cancel your wedding through serious illness, bereavement or even redundancy, a good poli-cy should cover the cancellation fees. Wedding insurance can't cover all eventualities, however. Don't expect big handouts if your day is ruined by bad weather or if one of you backs out of the wedding at the last minute.

- **Loss, theft or damage** – it's unlikely your cake maker will drop your cake outside the venue, or the photographer's equipment will be stolen from his/her car, complete with your wedding shots, but if something unforeseen like that does happen, you could receive compensation. It won't make up for the disappointment, but it will recoup some lost cash. Most policies will also cover things like outfits and rings, usually for a fixed period of, say, a week before the wedding.

- **Supplier disasters** – If suppliers go out of business after they have taken your deposits, or even the full amount, wedding insurance can often recover these costs for you or cover the cost or hiring new suppliers.

Rule of thumb 🎂

Some venues will insist you have public liability insurance. This is to cover yourself if you or one of your guests causes damage to the venue, or injures themselves or someone else. This form of insurance can be a good idea for your own peace of mind.

4

TIMING IS EVERYTHING: PLANNING THE DAY ITSELF

It doesn't matter what time you get married as long as it is between the hours of 8am and 6pm (apart from certain exceptions such as some Jewish weddings) but bear in mind the earlier in the day you choose, the longer you will have to entertain your guests and that might mean feeding them twice.

🌿 GETTING READY 🌿

Never underestimate how much time you need as a bride. Get your hair done first (providing you have a dress you can step into) then have your make-up applied. Don't try to apply make-up in your bridal gown and never try to paint your nails on the day – get them done the night before. Leave time for breakfast of some kind and a glass of champagne with your chief bridesmaid. People may want to stop by and wish you luck but this can get distracting so don't encourage too many people. If you want photos before you depart for the ceremony, aim to be ready for your close-up 20 minutes before your car arrives, so that you can take some deep breaths and practise that smile.

Stress buster

Traditionally, most if not all of your bridesmaids get ready at the same location as the bride. Never underestimate how long this can take if you're using the same make-up artist or hairdresser, and think twice about having your flower girls around. It can be easier to have them ready somewhere else.

TRAVELLING TO THE CEREMONY

Hopefully, you've stayed fairly close to the venue, so your transport provider should know exactly how long the journey takes. Even though it's a bride's prerogative to be late, leave on time so that you can spend those extra few minutes outside the venue touching up your make up, arranging your dress and soaking up the excitement – not sitting in traffic.

Pocket tip

Remember there may be other ceremonies scheduled after yours so being ridiculously late could mean you miss your slot – and it will have a knock on effect on the rest of the schedule, ie the time for your photos or drinks reception.

THE CEREMONY

This can be as short as 20 minutes at a register office to over an hour for a religious ceremony and full mass. It's tempting to try to catch up with everyone outside the venue, but if you're going on somewhere different for the reception, it's better to do that there, where everyone can also find a bathroom, a drink or somewhere to sit down. If you're having photos outside the church or ceremony venue, try to keep this reasonably short as well – around 15 minutes is a good amount of time.

Stress buster

Chew gum. Research shows that the physical action of chewing helps stimulate the part of the brain that reduces tension. But be careful where you put the gum before you make your big entrance. You don't want it on the bottom of your shoes while you're kneeling through prayers!

THE DRINKS RECEPTION

Once guests are settled at the reception venue, you can take your time over the photos, both group shots and your couple shots. Try to keep your drinks reception to around an hour to an hour and a half, otherwise people will drink lots of wine/champagne/cocktails on an empty stomach and it will go straight to their head, even if you are passing around nibbles.

THE WEDDING BREAKFAST

This is one timing you need to stick to, so make sure the best man is aware of when guests have to be marshalled to find their seats. If you agreed to sit down at 5pm, your caterers (hopefully) will have the first course ready at that time. Any delay now could be reflected in the quality of the food. Your caterers should have the experience to know how long it will take to prepare, serve and clear your chosen menu, so be guided by them.

THE SPEECHES

People often overestimate how long it takes to deliver a speech. Your dad may labour over his notes for weeks, but it could actually only take three or four minutes to read, especially if he's racing through because of nerves.

If you are going to present mums, bridesmaids and other people who have helped you with thank-you gifts during or straight after the speeches, don't forget to factor this into your time-frame. And make sure the presents themselves are near to hand before you stand up and start telling mum what a treasure she is. Nothing falls flatter than looking round helplessly to discover the bouquet you want to present is still in a bucket of water in the hotel's utility room!

Pocket tip
The best man usually speaks for the longest and received wisdom is that a speech lasting 15 minutes is usually enough. Aim to

leave around 30 minutes for all the speeches but don't be surprised if they are over in less time, unless you have some experienced raconteurs in your family!

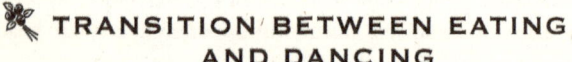

TRANSITION BETWEEN EATING AND DANCING

This is often the part of the day when guests mill around, not quite sure what to do, especially if the dining room is also the dancing room and the staff have to do a quick turnaround with the tables. If you think there will be half an hour to kill while the DJ or band set up, why not suggest that coffee is served in another room, lounge or bar or even on a terrace if it's warm enough. This is also a good time to roll out any entertainment you might have booked, ie a crowd magician or a caricaturist.

Sample schedule, although no wedding is typical so use this as a guideline only!

- Church ceremony 2pm

- Ceremony over by 2.40pm

- A few pictures outside church until around 3pm

- All cars leave for reception by 3.10pm

- Assuming reception venue is no more than 15 minutes away, bride and groom have 10 minutes to freshen up and are ready to greet guests by 3.30pm

- Drinks reception until 4.45pm, with everyone called to their seats for first course to be served by 5pm

- Allow till 7pm for food, speeches and coffee

5

SAYING I DO: THE CEREMONY

It may represent less than 10% of your overall day but your ceremony is still the most symbolic and legally binding part of the wedding day. That's not to say it's all business and no pleasure however, because this is where you have a captive audience, and everyone will be focusing on the music and the words, so it's worth investing some time to pick the right ones that reflect you as a couple.

KEEPING THE INTIMACY OF THE OCCASION

Your wedding ceremony is one of the most personal occasions of your life, yet – bizarrely   it is traditionally played out in a most public way. It's likely to be one of the rare (if not the *only*) occasions that you will stand up in front of everyone you hold most dear and declare your love for someone else. The thought can be pretty daunting if you are shy or not used to displaying feelings in public. Some couples like to restrict the ceremony itself to a very small select group of friends and family, and then invite all the workmates, university pals and distant cousins later. There is no fixed etiquette to this and if you decide to take this route, try not to let people make you feel you are somehow excluding them. They should still be honoured that you want them to join the celebration, if not the vows themselves.

CHURCH CEREMONIES

No two Church of England or Roman Catholic ceremonies are exactly the same, but there are general templates that can help you shape your ceremony. Here is a basic template for a church ceremony:

- Welcome and introduction by the minister

- First hymn

- The minister addresses the congregation to ask if anyone knows of any reason why the couple may not marry

- Declarations – you will be asked to promise that you will love, comfort, honour and protect each other, to which each of you answers 'I will'

- Exchange of vows, which have changed very little since the Middle Ages, and contain the section: 'To have and to hold, From this day forward, For better, for worse, For richer, for poorer . . .'

- Blessing of the ring/s, after which the groom or both of you says the words:

  'I give you this ring as a sign of our marriage . . .'

- Second hymn (if you are having three)

- The readings

- The minister's address

- Registration of the marriage – often while the choir sing or a soloist plays

- Prayers (and mass if you are having full communion)

- Minister's closing

POPULAR WEDDING HYMNS

The minister will want to approve your choice of music and hymns and may try to steer you away from certain lyrics which don't sit well at weddings (*Fight the Good Fight*, *For Those in Peril on the Sea* don't sit well with a romantic wedding!). Some ministers also draw the line at songs they see as too nationalistic – *I Vow to*

Thee My Country or *Jerusalem* may have been your favourite school hymn, but both have occasionally been banned from weddings by ministers as inappropriate. Let the minister guide you as to which verses to sing, too, as most guests struggle with 10 verses of any hymn!

1. **First hymn**. Pick something everyone knows to break the ice and warm up the vocal cords. How about: *O Jesus I have promised*, *All people that on Earth do dwell*, *Lord of all Hopefulness*, *Immortal Invisible*.

2. **Second hymn**. It's nice to have something gentle and reflective for after the vows and blessings. How about: *The Lord's my Shepherd* (23rd Psalm), *Morning has broken*, *Living Lord Make me a channel of your peace*, *Be still, for the presence of the Lord*, *Dear Lord and Father of Mankind*.

3. **Third hymn**. Choose a foot stomper of a hymn to finish with, something people can really belt out in celebration. How about: *At the name of Jesus*, *Praise my Soul*, *The King of Heaven*, *All things bright and beautiful*, *One more step along the World I go*, *Guide me O thou great redeemer*.

Pocket tip 🥂

Check if your church is covered by Christian Copyright Licensing (www.ccli.co.uk) which generally means you can video your ceremony although if you are having a professional filmmaker, you may need to get a Wedding Video Recording Licence (www.wvrl.co.uk). As always, ask your official for guidance.

🌿 CIVIL CEREMONIES 🌿

Register office ceremonies are designed to be quick and functional and are often the wedding of choice for second marriages (where one partner is divorced and unable to marry in church) followed by a blessing afterwards.

Pocket fact &

On the day there are two officials at any civil ceremony. One conducts the ceremony itself (the superintendent registrar or deputy superintendent registrar) and the other checks all your details on the paperwork a few minutes before the ceremony, then registers the marriage.

A ceremony at a licensed venue such as a hotel, castle or manor house means there is usually a little more scope to embellish your ceremony with your own vows. However, wherever you choose to get married, your civil ceremony is required, by law, to include some form of 'declaration' to say that you are free to marry: usually '*I declare that I know of no legal reason why I (name) may not be joined in marriage to (name)*' and will also include a contracting statement: '*I take you (name) to be my lawful wedded wife/husband*'. Outside of these statutory words, the registrar will offer you a variety of what are known as optional inserts – extra paragraphs of wording you can choose from – or you can put forward your own ideas.

Money saver

Make your own confetti cones using photocopied sheet music. Glue them into an open cone and decorate with mini coloured bows (the kind you would stick on a Christmas present) to match your colour scheme. If you have friends who grow roses, ask them to save fallen petals in the weeks leading up to the wedding and dry them flat in your airing cupboard to use as the confetti.

MUSIC FOR YOUR CEREMONY

When the minister or registrar asks 'have you thought about music?', most couples have to admit they haven't. In fact, many often start planning the disco playlist before thinking about the first few evocative bars that'll welcome their guests, announce the arrival of the bride and celebrate their first married walk back down the aisle together.

Pocket tip

Check every piece of music you want to play with your official. The law states that music for a civil ceremony must have 'no religious content whatsoever' although the definition of non-religious content is in the hands of the individual registrar. Some letter-of-the-law officials have banned Robbie Williams' Angels or Aretha Franklin's I Say A Little Prayer, others view them as an 'incidental reference to a god or deity in an essentially non-religious context' and are happy for them to be included.

There are a few different pieces of music you will need. Here's a brief explanation:

WELCOMING YOUR GUESTS

This is known as the Prelude music and tends to be something fairly unobtrusive, light and upbeat. If you're booking musicians, such as a string trio, ask them to play something welcoming and atmospheric, but bear in mind guests can arrive up to half an hour before the ceremony starts, so your musicians would need a lot of material on top of the music you have chosen for your arrival, signing the register etc. If you're making up a CD for the venue sound system, remember that modern songs are over in around three minutes so you would need up to a dozen songs. Classical music is generally longer, although listen to the disc all the way through in case there are gloomy or noisy movements further along in the opera or classical collection that are not very suitable for happy occasions!

THE PROCESSIONAL

Ask anyone to sing the bridal march and chances are they'll hum *Here Comes The Bride* better known as Wagner's Wedding March. But he's not the only composer in the classical top ten for the bride's arrival music (known in the trade as The Processional). This needs to be chosen with care, not just for the tune itself but with an eye on who's going to be playing it. The timing is crucial as you don't want an over-enthusiastic organist or pianist making you gallop down the aisle.

Pocket tip 🔔

The bride usually only takes between 30 and 60 seconds from her first appearance at the door of the venue to reaching the side of her groom, so you don't need a long piece.

SIGNING THE REGISTER

At church weddings this was traditionally a gentle piece of music in the background – however, don't choose something too gentle or guests will start to whisper and mutter over it. If you want to keep people's attention, consider staging a musical performance – a soloist singing, playing the flute or the piano maybe? If you have a church choir handy, see if they will perform a lovely aria like *Christ has no body now but yours* by George Ogden.

THE RECESSIONAL

At last, this is the triumphant 'yes, we did it!' moment so you can afford to choose something a bit grand or over the top if you want to. Equally, an unexpected chart hit or a song that means something to you both is equally okay at a civil ceremony, providing you run it past the registrar first.

Here are a few suggestions for the various musical interludes:

Welcoming your guests

Traditional

Prelude, Air and Gavotte, by Wesley
Nimrod from *Enigma Variations* by Elgar
Sheep may safely graze by Bach
Jesu, joy of man's desiring by Bach

Flower Duet from *Lakme* by Delibes
Romance Andante from *Eine Kleine Nachtmusik* by Mozart
Clair de Lune by Debussy
Air on a G String by Bach
Adagio for Strings by Samuel Barber
Nessun Dorma by Puccini

Contemporary

The mood and lyrics in all of these modern classics are perfect for a wedding. Some are more suited to the prelude or the register signing, others are perfect for the big final moment.

What a wonderful world by Louis Armstrong
We've only just begun by The Carpenters
How deep is your love by The Bird and the Bee
One day like this by Elbow
Overjoyed by Stevie Wonder
The Glasgow love theme by Craig Armstrong (from *Love Actually*)
I wanna grow old with you by Adam Sandler
You and me by Lifehouse
Truly madly deeply by Savage Garden
Isn't she lovely by Stevie Wonder
I say a little prayer by Aretha Franklin
The more I see you by Chris Montez
Make someone happy by Jimmy Durante
Someone like you by Van Morrison
Have I told you lately that I love you by Van Morrison or Rod Stewart
True love ways by Buddy Holly
We have all the time in the world by Louis Armstrong
Our love by Natalie Cole
Just like heaven by Katie Melua
Overjoyed by Stevie Wonder
At last by Etta James or Beyonce
The greatest day of our lives by Take That
This will be (our everlasting love) by Natalie Cole
From this moment on by Shania Twain
Looks like we made it by Barry Manilow
The best is yet to come by Tony Bennett
L.O.V.E. by Nat King Cole

Pocket tip

Agree with your organist or soloist how quickly the music is going to be played. Your idea of a gentle stroll down the aisle on dad's arm could turn into a gallop at the hands of an over-enthusiastic musician. Better still record it on a CD so that you can practice walking in your heels and even your dress.

Processional

Traditional

The Wedding March from *Lohengrin* by Wagner
Trumpet Voluntary from *The Prince of Denmark's March* by J Clarke
Music for the Royal Fireworks by Handel
Hornpipe in D from *The Water Music* by Handel
Entrance of the Queen of Sheba by Handel
Trumpet Tune in D Major by Purcell
Canon in D by Pachelbel
Te Deum by Charpentier
Grand March from *Aida* by Verdi
Spring from *The Four Seasons* by Vivaldi

Pocket fact

Actress Sophie Thompson chose the music from The Magic Roundabout when she walked down the aisle in 1995 to marry musician Richard Lumsden. Her unusual choice was to honour the memory of her late father, Eric Thompson who wrote and narrated the original 1960s children's classic.

Do it your way

Do you need a bridesmaid to carry your train? Few brides do these days but most still make their entrance with the brides-maids following in their wake. There's actually no rule that says you have to do it in this order. Make your entrance the American way and follow your flower girls (ideally scattering petals) and your bridesmaids so that it builds up to your own big moment.

Signing the register

Traditional

Ave Maria by Schubert
Jesu Joy of Man's Desiring by Bach
Nocturne from *String Quartet* by Borodin
Clair de Lune by Debussy
Christ has no body now but yours by David Ogden
Air on a G String by Bach
Sheep May Safely Graze by Bach
The Lord Bless you and keep you by Rutter

The Recessional

Traditional

The Rejoicing from *Music for the Royal Fireworks* by Handel
Hallelujah Chorus from *The Messiah* by Handel
Ode to Joy by Beethoven
Air from *Water Music Suite* by Handel
Trumpet Tune and Air by Henry Purcell
Wedding March from *A Midsummer Night's Dream* by Mendelssohn
Finale from *Symphony No. 1* by Widor
Carillon De Westminster by Vierne
Pomp and Circumstance March No 4 by Elgar
Fanfare by Whitlock

Pocket tip 🥂

Most registrars and ministers encourage a congratulatory round of applause once the ceremony is over, but guests are often stumped over whether to clap after a performance by a soloist or a choir. Check with your official and if he or she thinks that would be appropriate, ask your best man to brief the ushers to start the applause. There's nothing worse than a few lukewarm claps . . .

TRUE OR FALSE: SOME COMMON CEREMONY MYTHS

The bride has to arrive on the arm of her father or another male relative.

False. This is a custom not a requirement and the bride is free to walk down the aisle with her mother, best friend, husband-to-be, son or daughter or even by herself if she likes. As always, it is best to check with the official at your wedding about your ideas to break with tradition just so he or she knows your plans.

The wedding official can dictate what a bride wears.

Partly true. Certain religious officials may try to object to bare shoulders or low-cut gowns on the grounds that it is unseemly in a place of worship. This is down to the individual minister rather than church policy, which is why it is a good idea to feel comfortable with your minister and air any concerns in advance of the big day.

A groom has to have a best man to carry the rings.

False. Again this is tradition. Legally you only need five people at a wedding – an official, a bride, a groom and two witnesses. And the witnesses do not even have to be people you know. You can drag them in off the street if you want to go completely solo!

Religious music is not allowed at a civil ceremony.

True. The background music, readings and vows at a civil wedding must have no religious content or reference whatsoever. For couples who have chosen a civil ceremony because they have no faith, this is not usually as problem. However, if you want to include some Christmas carols at a winter wedding, for instance, it's usually not a problem provided the carol singing is separate from the actual ceremony – preferably in a separate room or location, after the registrar has gone.

We both have to exchange rings.

False. Actually neither of you has to exchange rings if you don't want to – it's a tradition not a legal requirement. Although it is common practice at modern weddings, some couples also choose to exchange other items of jewellery such as lockets or pendants, as they are worn close to the heart, or bangles (unbroken circles, just like a wedding band).

Three traditions from around the world

1. The Arrhae ceremony at a **Filipino** wedding involves the priest dropping 13 coins into the groom's cupped hands, which he in turn drops into the bride's hands cupped below his. The trickle of coins represents sharing and good luck for the future.
2. Ducks are thought to mate for life which is why some **Korean** weddings include ducks in the wedding procession.
3. In both **Italy** and **Spain**, the groom's tie is considered lucky and is sometimes cut into pieces during the reception and auctioned off to raise funds for the couple's honeymoon.

WRITING YOUR OWN VOWS

Whatever your style of ceremony, you're required to repeat the statutory declarations set down by law but couples are increasingly choosing to embellish their vows with a few lines of their own making. Providing you run through everything with the official in advance, this shouldn't be a problem. What might cause you headaches is finding the right words to share your feelings with an audience on what is already an emotional day.

Pocket fact

Caitlin Hallnan and Richard Lewis only gave friends and family three weeks notice for their wedding in Birkenhead Town Hall, which meant some people from the US couldn't make their day. So the couple devised a canny way to involve everyone, by repeating their vows into a mobile phone!

WHERE TO START

You won't get it right first time so just brainstorm together with as many ideas as possible, then sift through them, choose the most appropriate to you and gradually mould your special words into shape. Write down a long list of words that you associate with a happy marriage and choose your favourites.

Concentrate on key themes like:

Commitment: trust; loyalty; fidelity; reliability; responsibility; friendship
Happiness: joy; peace; kindness; compassion; understanding
Share: grow; encourage; support
Protect: care; cherish; nurture

Pocket tip

If one or both of you has a child, this is the perfect opportunity to add in some personalised vows recognising the new start for the whole family. Ask your official whether it would be possible for the child/children to step forward (or at least stand up) and repeat the vows with you.

CHOOSING YOUR READINGS

At a religious ceremony you will be asked to include at least one reading with religious reference but you may be able to have a second non-religious reading, which could be anything from an extract from *Captain Corelli's Mandolin*, *Love is a temporary madness . . .*, to *Wherever I Am, There's Always Pooh . . .* (*Us Two* by AA Milne from *Now We Are Six*). Remember though that for a civil ceremony, no readings can refer to God, angels, heaven or have any religious connotations whatsoever.

Other ways to make your celebration unique include reading lines of poetry to each other, or asking the official to include famous quotations, proverbs or pieces of philosophy that you particularly like into the welcome or the address.

POPULAR BIBLE READINGS

Genesis 2: 18–25 The Lord God said, 'It is not good for the man to be alone . . .'

Song of Solomon 2: 10–14 My beloved spoke and said to me, 'Arise, my darling, my beautiful one, come with me . . .'

Ecclesiastes 4: 9–12 Two are better than one because they have a good return for their labour . . .

Mark 10: 6–9, 13–16 At the beginning of creation God made them male and female . . .

1 Corinthians 13: 1–3 If I speak in human or angelic tongues but do not have love, I am only a resounding gong or a clanging cymbal . . .

1 Corinthians 13: 4–10 Love is patient, love is kind. It does not envy, it does not boast, it is not proud . . .

1 Corinthians 13: 11–13 When I was a child I thought like a child, I talked like a child, I reasoned like a child . . .

Psalm 84 How lovely is your dwelling place . . . Even the sparrow has found a home and the swallow a nest for herself . . .

NON BIBLICAL READINGS FOR A RELIGIOUS CEREMONY

Marriage by Khalil Gilbran
She Walks in Beauty by Lord Byron
Yes, I'll Marry You by Pam Ayres
Love is a Temporary Madness from *Captain Corelli's Mandolin* by Louis de Bernieres

POPULAR READINGS FOR CIVIL CEREMONIES

Love and Friendship by Emily Bronte
Married Love by Kuan Tao Sheng
A Dedication to my Wife by TS Eliot
If Thou Must Love Me by Elizabeth Barrett Browning
Sonnet 116 'Let me not to the marriage of two minds admit impediment . . .' by William Shakespeare
The First Day by Christina Rossetti
O Tell Me The Truth About Love by WH Auden

Anon but not forgotten

Many lovely verses and readings have been passed down through the ages without anyone knowing where they began. Here are a couple of examples:

This I can promise
I cannot promise you a lifetime of sunshine
I cannot promise riches, wealth or gold
I cannot promise you an easy pathway
That leads away from change or growing old
But I can promise all my heart's devotion
A smile to chase away your tears of sorrow
A love that's ever true and ever growing
A hand to hold in yours through each tomorrow

What is love?
Sooner or later we begin to understand that love is more
Than verses on valentines and romance in the movies.
We begin to know that love is here and now, real and true, the most important thing in our lives.
For love is the creator of our favourite memories and the foundation of our fondest dreams.

Stress buster

To combat those butterflies in the tummy eat a good breakfast. Not only will it regulate your blood sugar and boost energy levels, but digesting it gives your system something else to think about other than to pump adrenaline around the body.

Pets at weddings

There's a growing trend for couples to include cherished pets at their weddings. This includes brides riding to their ceremony on their horse or having dogs as ring bearers. There have even been stories of domestic pigs being decorated with a pretty ribbon and coming to the ball and trained owls swooping down to deliver the wedding bands! You only have to look on the internet for companies selling doggy tuxedos and sparkly crystal collars to see that a mini industry has grown up around the idea. Most liberal registrars and ministers are happy to go along with the idea provided it doesn't interfere with the solemnity of the occasion but this really is something you have to discuss with your official first – in detail.

If you have your heart set on being escorted down the aisle by your beloved Labrador remember that veterinary advice on including pets at weddings suggests that you limit it to the ceremony only and nominate someone to take responsibility of the animal during the service. Even the most placid dog can get agitated in an unfamiliar location surrounded by lots of noise and strangers.

6

THE DRINKS RECEPTION

After the serious business of the vows and rings, it's time to party and, for the bride in particular, it's the first opportunity to catch up with all the guests. The more traditional way is for the couple to form a receiving line with their parents and maybe the chief bridesmaid and best man. In its favour, this is one way of ensuring you meet everyone at least for a few seconds, however a receiving line can also become exhausting on the face muscles, repetitive because people usually can't think of anything very original to say other than 'lovely service' or 'you look beautiful' and it can be slow.

TIME TO MINGLE

Phew! The scary bit of making an entrance walking down the aisle and repeating your vows is over. You might think this is time for you to relax, but everyone is going to want a little part of you on your big day so be prepared for lots of smiling and small talk. Remember, the groom has the advantage of meeting most of the guests before the ceremony. He's had everyone tease him about how smart he looks and whether he's taken the price tag off his new shoes already. Now most people are going to want to chat to the bride.

TIPS FOR WORKING A ROOM

- If you have 90 guests to get round, devoting just a minute to each would take an hour and a half so be realistic! Weave your way around the room with a permanent air of being on your way somewhere; this way you can say 'hi' to some people, wave to others and mouth 'see you in a bit?' to people you know are going to dominate your time.

- If people are happily chatting away in big groups, leave them to it – you can catch up with them later – and turn your attention to single friends or couples who may not know many other people. (Ask the best man to look out for guests who are looking excluded, too, as part of his duties.) Lone guests often just need a gentle nudge in the direction of another.

- Have some ready prepared anecdotes handy. Most guests are fairly unoriginal when it comes to talking to brides, even someone they've known for years. Expect lots of 'you look beautiful. . .', 'lovely service' and 'you were lucky with the weather'.

- Put yourself first. No matter how much you love someone, if they are boring you rigid, move on. It's your wedding and you're allowed to be selfish!

Money saver

In September 2009, two Church of England bishops launched an appeal for more couples to hold low-key and value-for-money receptions in the church premises themselves. It's a logical step, said the Bishops of London and Hereford, as 80% of cathedral and church buildings are listed as being of architectural or historic interest and many would make ideal locations. One example given was St Laurence's in Reading, Berkshire, a 12th century church with a modern glass mezzanine level above the nave which is popular with newlyweds.

🌸 THE RECEIVING LINE – MAKE IT 🌸 WORK FOR YOU

Here are a few dos and don'ts to help you greet your guests without being stuck for hours:

- DO keep the number of people in the receiving line to a minimum. Unless your parents are hosting the occasion and desperately want the traditional meet-and-greet format, keep it to just bride and groom (and maybe best man to keep everyone moving along at a cracking pace).

- DON'T make people queue outside the venue before they have had a chance to go to the loo or grab a drink. Have someone hold a tray of glasses at the beginning of the line so that guests can sip bubbly or Pimm's while they are waiting.

- DO think about having a distraction along the way. If you have a lot of guests and the line is going to take a while, a display of photos of you both as children, or pictures of yourselves with all your guests, gives everyone something to chat about and breaks the line as they are queuing.

Pocket fact 🐚

Nervous about all that kissing and embarrassing nose bumping on the receiving line? Scientists have concluded that 80% of men and women automatically turn their heads to the right when they kiss friends socially — irrespective of whether they are right or left handed.

🌿 WHAT TO DRINK? 🌿

Most wedding celebrations begin with some form of drinks reception, either while the couple are greeting guests or while they are having photographs taken, and it's a chance for people to mingle. Make sure you have some nibbles available too, because for an afternoon wedding, most guests are too busy getting ready or driving to the venue to bother with lunch and the alcohol will go straight to their bloodstream.

Pocket tip 🔔

Allow at least a litre of mineral water per person as people can get through at least this much during the course of a day, especially during hot weather.

Don't forget plenty of soft drinks for children, drivers and non-drinkers. Sparkling water and orange juice can get boring, so why not ask your venue to make up a decent non-alcoholic fruit punch?

Money saver

Traditionally wedding breakfasts started with champagne, but this can work out to be expensive if you're on a budget. Shop around for a decent fizz substitute (such as Prosecco from Italy, Cava from Spain) and if you're worried your guests will notice the difference — which they probably won't — mix it with crème de cassis to make Kir Royale, fresh orange juice to make Bucks Fizz or peach puree for a Bellini cocktail.

WELCOME COCKTAILS

If you don't fancy the champagne route, why not serve a punch or a signature cocktail? Whatever you do, don't serve sherry. That went out with pounds, shillings and pence! Here are a few suggestions:

Mai Tai

For a taste of the Caribbean, follow this recipe (per serving): 2oz Jamaican rum, 1oz fresh lime juice, 1oz orange Curacao.

Mulled red wine

This goes down really well at a winter wedding. For every bottle of red wine you use add ¼ pint of apple juice, the zest of half a lemon and half an orange, a couple of slices of peeled orange, one cinnamon stick, and three–four cloves. Don't forget to heat NOT boil the wine, as this cooks out all the alcohol! For an autumn wedding you can do a version with white wine, too, adding some apples and honey to taste.

Pimm's Classic

This is perfect for a summer marquee wedding. For every bottle of Pimm's you use add three times the amount of lemonade (or for an extra kick, add one part ginger ale to two parts lemonade). Decorate with orange, cucumber and mint. For a winter twist, mix three bottles of warm apple juice to each bottle of Pimm's and decorate with slices of apple, orange and lemon.

Money saver

If you're hoping to go off on a booze cruise and supply your own wine or champagne, check with your venue about corkage. If they're going to charge you per bottle, you may find you won't save much, if anything, but some venues will agree a corkage charge per person, which could make it worth your while.

Pocket tip 🥂

You can expect to get around five glasses from a bottle of wine and six from a bottle of bubbly. If you're serving champagne before the meal, allow at least two glasses per person, even for designated drivers. Although some people will be driving later, most choose to have their legal limit quota at the beginning of the reception, when the fizz is flowing, and move on to soft drinks later.

🌿 NIBBLES TO SOAK UP THE 🌿 CHAMPAGNE

While your guests are sipping their champagne try serving some of the following nibbles:

- Parmesan bread sticks
- Mini vegetable spring rolls
- Mini vegetable samosas
- Wild mushroom tartlets
- Onion bhajis
- Mini bruschetta (toasted ciabatta with tomato, mozzarella and basil)
- Smoked mackerel pâté on toasted walnut bread
- Smoked salmon blinis
- Mini Yorkshire puddings with rare roast beef

Pocket tip 🥂

For a drinks reception of one and a half to two hours, allow between 8 and 14 bite-size canapés per person.

SWEET CANAPÉS

These are a good idea if you're not having a formal seated breakfast. Try serving:

- Caramelised fruit skewers
- Pannacottas in shot glasses
- Mini ice-cream cones filled with lemon sorbet
- Mini white chocolate cups
- Chocolate brownies
- Strawberries dipped in chocolate

Stress buster

Try to keep most of your canapés vegetarian if possible. It makes life easier for the servers, as well as your vegetarian guests, and most meat-eaters like vegetarian nibbles just as well as meat or fish — they probably won't even notice!

RETRO CANAPÉS FOR A 70S THEMED PARTY – SERVE WITH PLENTY OF ABBA!

- Cheese and pineapple. Update it with chunks of blue cheese and mix in with the same number of skewers of mozzarella or halloumi with cherry tomatoes and silverskin onions.

- Vol au vents. Avoid tiny tasteless prawns and fill with mixed sauté mushrooms instead.

- Slices of pork pie and mini scotch eggs.

- Cheese straws.

Pocket tip

Your guests are dressed up in all their finery so don't make them eat oily canapés or anything that flakes, oozes or drips. If you want to serve olives provide cocktail sticks so people don't get greasy fingers. The best canapés are one mouthful in size and don't contain too many foreign bodies (ie spinach, watercress, rocket) that can stick in people's teeth.

7

THE WEDDING BREAKFAST

You'll feed your guests at least once depending on the time of your ceremony and the catering will eat up (pardon the pun) a large portion of your budget. Most caterers agree that the best menus use the best produce – ideally organic or free range, locally grown and fresh – so keep it simple and seasonal by doing less, but doing it well.

🌿 WEDDING BREAKFAST 🌿 TRADITIONS

- Once the best man (or master of ceremonies) has marshalled everyone to their seats, it's traditional for the bride and groom to enter the dining room last to cheers and a round of applause. It's a nice touch if guests can be standing when they enter and only sit down after the happy couple.

- If you're planning to say grace before dinner – maybe the minister from the ceremony is joining you for the meal – it's helpful if this is printed at the top of the menu (if you're having one) so that people know it's coming before they dive into the bread basket.

- Traditionally men keep their jackets on until a) the groom removes his or b) the main course is being cleared. This is something younger generations may not be aware of, so to avoid confusion get the best man to tap a glass, stand up and quickly say something like, 'we're dispensing with tradition gentlemen, so please feel free to remove your jackets'. This usually gives rise to peals of laughter from the rugby club table who took theirs off with the first glass of champagne!

 WHAT ARE YOUR OPTIONS?

FORMAL SILVER SERVICE

The seated and served option will usually be the most expensive because you're paying for a team of waiting staff to get all three courses out at more or less the same time.

Good for: marquee receptions or venues where the tables are quite tightly packed and a buffet arrangement would be too chaotic.

Bad for: socialising with people at other tables.

SEATED BUFFET

A little more relaxed but still with a structured seating plan. Usually less costly than a three-course meal as fewer staff are needed.

Good for: offering guests a wider selection of dishes. Good for winter weddings when you can serve big pots of warming casseroles, chillis or curries.

Bad for: figuring out if people have had enough to eat.

INFORMAL BUFFET

A relaxed sit-where-you-can option which you can hold indoors or out, and where people can graze and eat when they like.

Good for: parties where a lot of people know each other.

Bad for: lots of small groups, couples, or singles who've never met before as people tend to sit alone among strangers and feel polarised.

BARBECUES AND HOG ROASTS

Similarly relaxed but make sure you have a covered area in case of rain!

Good for: summer weddings or country fete-style themes. Hire a professional company and get them to serve the least-messy options available – ie souvlaki, steak and tuna which can be eaten with a knife and fork, not hand held burgers that will ooze ketchup over everyone's best clothes!

Bad for: unexpected bad weather, or messy eaters!

Pocket fact ❦

Some couples just can't face the whole three-course-meal and seating plan palaver. Newlyweds Paula Traill and Simon Hand spent just £70 on burgers and fries, all washed down with strawberry milkshake, when they entertained 20 of their closest family and friends at the branch of McDonald's opposite the Stockport register office in Greater Manchester.

HOT NEW IDEAS FOR ALTERNATIVE WEDDING BREAKFASTS

These new trends are growing increasingly popular at receptions:

Food stalls

Rather than the 'try-to-please everyone' buffet, wedding caterers are increasingly being asked for themed food stalls. These could include sweet or savoury crepes made to order, sushi bars or sea food bars complete with cockles, mussels and jellied eels. Just think of it as the same idea as a dessert trolley or a cheese table. Some couples are even ditching the wedding cake for a lavish cheese station instead.

Canapé bars

Food as theatre is another increasingly popular idea – why not have a canapé chef standing behind a bar with a selection of tempting ingredients preparing canapés such as blinis while people watch and wait. It's a good talking point for guests to break the ice and people often find it so fascinating, they forget to drink the champagne quite so quickly.

Bring your own buffet

This is where everyone brings an individual dish and places it on a shared buffet table. The idea works well at a country-fete or picnic-style summer wedding. But if you think your guests might find it a bit too much to provide their own meal on top of the expense of finding an outfit/wedding gift/hotel etc why not restrict it to bring-a-cupcake where everyone bakes or at least ices a special cupcake for you which are all displayed on a tiered stand.

Pocket tip 🥂

Buffets can save money because you don't need high numbers of waiting staff, but you will need some staff on hand to help with carving, to replenish empty bowls of salads or simply explain to guests what the dishes are and what ingredients are in certain recipes. This is particularly important for vegetarians or guests with food allergies.

Celeb watch

You might think the Hollywood A-listers always celebrate their lavish weddings with feasts of champagne and caviar. Not so:

- *Speed actress **Sandra Bullock** put southern-fried chicken and barbecued ribs on the menu for her wedding to TV star Jess James.*
- *Pretty Woman **Julia Roberts** and Danny Moder also stocked up on ketchup serving guests hot dogs and hamburgers.*
- *When Bourne Identity star **Matt Damon** tied the knot with Luciana Barrosa at New York City Hall the happy couple and a handful of friends allegedly tucked into pretzels and Jewish potato dumplings called knishes from a Big Apple street vendor.*

🌿 CHOOSING A MENU 🌿

If you're going for a traditional three-course seated breakfast, you could save yourself a few pennies by serving a cold starter that is already plated and at the tables when guests sit down. In addition to the lower expense the staff will appreciate not having to get 100+ bowls of warm soup on to the tables at once.

When it comes to the main course, popular choices still tend to be chicken, lamb, beef and salmon, because they are universally popular across generations – and they don't have to be boring in the hands of a creative caterer.

In the last few years trios of desserts have become increasingly popular, as has a return to gastro-pub favourites like sticky toffee pudding. Ask your caterer if they can give you two options for each course which guests can tick off when they return their RSVP. This cuts down the worry about having to please everyone.

Stress buster

Avoid waiting staff having to ask 'who's having the salmon. . .?' with a colour coded system. Buy a bag of coloured sticky stars (the sort teachers use in infant schools) and stick them on the table cloth to the left of each place setting (at the top near the spoons) to show everyone's choice, ie blue for fish starter, red for meat course, green for vegetarian etc.

Here are a few ideas to inspire your menu:

Cold starter ideas

- Mediterranean breads with oils and dips of hummus and salsas, olives, prosciutto, sun blush tomatoes and tomato, mozzarella and basil (tricolore) salads
- Two types of melon with Parma ham
- Chicken liver or pork terrine with seasonal chutneys
- Seafood cocktail
- Gazpacho soup or another consommé
- Smoked salmon with horseradish and green salad

Warm starter ideas

- Mini pasta dish with clams (not spaghetti, think of the outfits!)
- Soup (asparagus or fresh pea for spring, watercress for summer, pumpkin and parmesan for autumn, spicy beetroot for winter)
- Warm salads of duck breast, bacon, or chicken livers

Main course ideas

- Herb crusted fillet of beef with Dauphinoise potatoes
- Seared sea bass with lemon and capers
- Salmon with a pesto crust with couscous
- Chicken or poussin with garden vegetables
- Cumberland bangers and mash

Vegetarian options

- Mediterranean roast vegetable terrine

- Goat's cheese and chive soufflé

- Wild mushroom risotto (consider pumpkin for an autumn wedding)

- Meze of hummus, grilled courgettes with feta, mini kebabs of cherry tomatoes and peppers

- Fresh pasta using seasonal vegetables (primavera with asparagus for spring, pea, zucchini and artichoke for summer)

Popular puds

- Duo or white and dark chocolate mousse with berry compote
- Lemon meringue pie
- Eton mess (meringue, berries and cream)
- Lemon tart
- Rich chocolate torte
- Summer pudding

Pocket fact &

No-one is sure how the 'wedding breakfast' got its name. Theories include the fact that weddings were traditionally held in the morning or that it's the first meal you share as husband and wife, in the same way that breakfast is the first meal of the day.

THE SEATING PLAN

This is often the point where even the most organised bridezilla, sits down for a little weep. Who to put where? How to keep everyone happy? What to do with guests who don't like each other?

The traditional top table seating is (left to right) chief bridesmaid, groom's father, bride's mother, groom, bride, bride's father, groom's mother, best man. However this can soon get complicated with step-parents, in which case the extra parent/s are sometimes invited to sit beside their spouses or added to the end on either side of the chief bridesmaid and best man. If you're finding it hard to work out who should sit on the top table – particularly if you have divorced parents on either or both sides – don't even try. Ask both sets of parents to host their own table of friends and family, and order a little sweetheart table for yourselves. A popular trend from America, this is a table for two which you can have placed right in the middle of the hall, or even moved to different spots of the venue for different courses, so that everyone gets a chance to sit near the happy couple. You could also try making the top table a round table so that there isn't so much focus on who is sitting next to who.

Pocket tip 🔔

When you view your empty venue, imagine it full of people. Would you be better off with small or big tables? If space is tight, lots of tables can be a squeeze because more chairs have to back on to (and bash into) others. Large tables require less chair room, although small tables are useful in a narrow or unusually-shaped area with recesses or pillars.

TEN TIPS FOR THE PERFECT SEATING PLAN

1. Ringfence different groups of guests – bride's family, groom's family, childhood, school or college friends, sports mates, work colleagues – then colour-code them according to whether people know other individuals or groups and whether you can split them up.

2. While you're moving loved ones around the table plan like chess pieces remember everyone has feelings. Be careful who you stick at the furthest table at the back or beside the toilets.

3. If you're not having a conventional top table, think about where the people giving the speeches are going to sit. Will everyone be able to hear them?

4. If there are a lot of windows or French doors at your reception location, visit the venue at the same time of day you plan to be there and try to make sure people are not going to be blinded by early evening sunlight.

5. Try to avoid sitting elderly relatives too far from the bathroom or putting children's tables too close to the exit where they can wander off. Also avoid positioning tables too near the kitchen / serving area, as there's often a lot of shouting, door banging and crashing pots and pans when food is served.

6. Sitting like-minded people together is more important than making the seating a strict boy-girl-boy arrangement. Why not ask your best man to announce a system that sees every other person move two seats to the right after every course. That way, if your seating plan isn't totally perfect, at least your guests are not stuck talking to the same person throughout the whole meal.

7. Numbering tables creates a pecking order and someone is bound to take offence! Give your tables names instead. You could name them after places you've visited together, bands you love, your favourite pubs, famous painters, the choices are endless.

8. When making your seating chart remember to include guests' first initials, otherwise all the Mr Smiths will try to sit at the same place!

9. Although it can be fun to try and play matchmaker at your wedding, don't make it too obvious by sitting all your single friends together.

10. Make sure you check all the names on the seating chart against all of the RSVPs, just to make sure you don't leave anyone out!

Wise words

Proverbs from around the world are a wonderful way to celebrate different cultures. You could print them in a script font, laminate them and use as centrepieces on your reception tables. Here are a few suggestions:

- *The gold of one's heart is far more precious than the gold of one's purse* **(Chinese)**
- *No road is long with good company* **(Turkish)**
- *When two spiders unite they can tie up a lion* **(Ethiopian)**
- *Shared joy is a double joy. Shared sorrow is half a sorrow* **(Swedish)**

Pocket fact ✿

Escort cards are an idea from America gaining popularity in the UK. As guests enter for dinner they pick up little cards telling them which table to sit on but not which seat, which means people can suit themselves. Good for groups of friends – not so good for single people who don't know many people.

🐝 THE SPEECHES 🐝

There comes a point in every wedding when someone taps a fork against a glass and asks for hush. For the father of the bride, it is the moment to be proud, for the groom it's the moment to be sentimental and for the best man it's time to be funny. Speeches are traditionally done after the wedding meal and during the coffee, but it's increasingly popular to hold the speeches earlier, during the drinks reception. This works particularly well if speakers can stand on a staircase, a little stool or a low wall and everyone just crowds around, so that everyone can see and hear them. It also means the speakers can enjoy their meal without the nervous build-up. It also makes more sense in terms of the father of the bride's speech which is essentially to 'welcome' everyone there on the day.

Pocket tip 🥂

The father of the bride usually opens the speeches (or an uncle or brother fulfilling the FOB role), followed by the groom and then the best man. If the bride is speaking, she generally speaks between the groom and best man.

WHAT MAKES A GOOD SPEECH?

- **Emotion**. A good speech needs to recognise the significance of the day and balance sentimentality with schmaltz. Guests want to see the FOB or the groom visibly moved by emotion, but not sobbing uncontrollably.

- **Relevance**. Stick to sections of the couple's lives that everyone will be familiar with, such as how they met. Avoid lengthy in-jokes about days at university or long-winded stories about people who are not present.

- **Structure**. A successful speech has a beginning, a middle and an end. Rambling and repetition quickly switches an audience off.

FAVOURITE ONE-LINERS

Father of the bride

'It's been a long time since I used to read this little girl a story at bedtime. Now that role has passed to [groom's name] and I just know that every story from now on is going to have a happy ending.'

'When I watched my beautiful [bride's name] getting married today, I felt a lump in my throat and a tear in my eye. She may be all grown-up and independent, but she'll always be my little girl – the same little girl who drew wonderful stick-men paintings of me . . . at a time when I still had hair!'

'I know the old tradition of a father "giving away" his daughter has gone out of fashion. And quite right too I think. I could never give away [bride's name]. She's far too precious and priceless!'

Groom

'I don't want to embarrass her by saying this but I've never seen [wife's name] look so beautiful, so composed, so radiant and so . . . [looks at wife] what was the last one darling?'

'Mr & Mrs xxxx, you're not losing a daughter today, but you are losing any chance you ever had of her marrying into money!'

Best man

'I'm under strict instructions to avoid all mention of the stag weekend today. So I will. What goes on tour, stays on tour . . . including the luggage which we haven't got back yet!'

'I've known this guy for many years and I've never seen him so, um, what's the word . . . worried!'

Stress buster

Positive thinking can be very useful in controlling nerves. Before making a speech, conjure up an image in your mind of how you want it to look. Are your guests clapping, smiling, laughing at your joke, dabbing away a tear? See, you knew you could do it!

TRADITIONAL TOASTS – WHO, WHEN AND WHAT?

It's bad luck to toast with an empty glass so make sure the serving staff sees everyone is topped up before you start the speeches. There are no hard and fast rules about toasts although, traditionally, the father of the bride proposes a toast to the happy couple, the groom responds by toasting the bridesmaids and the best man rounds off proceedings by toasting the couple once more. In practice, it's not unusual for the bride, the groom's father or the matron of honour to stand up (usually before the best man) and propose a toast – maybe to someone who has passed away, couldn't come on the day or to another family member who played a big role in the celebration.

Pocket tip

When someone proposes the toast 'to the bride and groom' the newlyweds in question actually stay in their seats. They can sip from their glasses along with everyone else though!

8

THE RECEPTION

After the wedding breakfast is finished it's time to indulge in some time honoured wedding traditions, including cutting the cake and having your first dance as man and wife.

THE CAKE

THE ORIGINS OF THE WEDDING CAKE

There are as many theories on the origins of the wedding cake as there are cultures around the world, but most have something to do with fertility rites and a bride's rite of passage from virgin to married woman. Some of the most popular include:

Ancient Rome
Grains were traditionally linked to a woman's fertility and Roman wedding guests believed that sprinkling the newlyweds with cakes made from barley and wheat would help them on their way to their first born.

Ancient Egypt
As Egyptian newlyweds made their way home after their ceremony, family members would shower them with green wheat to wish them fruit in the marriage bed.

Celtic
At traditional Celtic weddings shortbread would be crumbled over the heads of the groom and bride as they came out of the church and unmarried guests would jostle to collect the crumbs – like catching the bride's bouquet, it was considered a good omen for being the next to get married.

Mediaeval England

There's no evidence of a central cake being a big part of a wedding celebration, but one tradition that grew up around this time involved piling sweet buns high into a tower and then challenging the groom to kiss the bride above the tower without knocking them over.

Pocket fact &

With post-war rationing still in force, the Queen's official wedding cake in 1947 was made by McVitie and Price Ltd using ingredients given to her Majesty and Prince Philip by the Australian Girl Guide organisation!

St Bride's inspires brides

The creator of the modern tiered-style wedding cake is thought to be an 18th century baker called William Rich. He was inspired by the way Sir Christopher Wren layered the spire in ever decreasing tiers on St Bride's Church in London's Fleet Street and used the shape for a cake for his daughter's wedding. And voila! Brides have been following the St Bride's cake design ever since.

CUTTING THE CAKE

Cutting the cake has come to be a set piece and an obligatory photo. Traditionally slices of fruit cake were individually boxed and posted to guests unable to make it to the wedding and a tier was kept in a sealed container to be used to celebrate the Christening of the couple's first child. Today, as more and more couples steer away from the heavy fruit cake idea at the end of a meal, the posted cake is a bit of a rarity.

- Traditionally, the couple cuts the cake together as it's the first 'task' they do together as man and wife.

- If either family has connections with the military, it's fun to make the moment even more ceremonial by using a sword, but make sure you run though how you're both going to wield the weapon beforehand, or you might do your cake – or yourselves – some damage!

- When the moment comes, the groom puts his right hand over the bride's and they cut the bottom tier together, remembering to look up for the cameras at the same time.

- Everyone likes to take a photo of the cake-cutting moment so spare a thought for what's in the background before you decide which way to stand. Don't have your wonderful moment marred by an emergency exit sign, an unsightly plug or the arrow to the toilets!

- It's also an old custom for the bride and groom to feed a piece to each other to symbolise sharing, but this could be risky with one of the increasingly popular chocolate torte-style cakes. Think of the dress!

- Cake-cutting is not obligatory and if you're having an alternative idea such as a tiered cupcakes or a croquenbouche (a traditional French tower of little choux pastries rather like profiteroles), you may decide to plate the first couple of cupcakes for your guests instead.

Pocket tip 🥂

How much cake feeds how many people? Here's a quick rule of thumb: a 12 inch tier of rich chocolate torte-style cake or sponge cake should serve around 50 guests, whereas the same sized fruit cake would go a lot further — probably serving over 100.

Money saver

Dessert cakes — chocolate, lemon sponge, carrot or a mix of all three — are very popular at weddings now, rather than the traditional, heavier fruit cake. Save yourself the cost of an entire pudding course by ordering a luxury dessert cake, cutting it before the meal, then have your catering staff slice it during the main course and serving it with cream or berries.

🐝 DECORATING YOUR 🐝
RECEPTION VENUE

The overall wav-factor of your reception will probably features as much in your wedding daydreams as your dress. Here are just a few ideas to help you make the dream a reality.

One of the easiest ways to decorate a room is to follow a simple colour scheme for balloons, napkins, tablecloths etc. Obviously you can have any colour you like in any season, but here are some tried-and-tested colour palettes that work every time:

- **Spring:** pale green and white, lemon and pale blue, cherry blossom pink, peach and apricot with a pale mocha.

- **Summer:** pinks of all shades from powder through to rhubarb to fuchsia and even neon pink (the brighter pinks work well as highlights to a monochrome black colour scheme). Also lilacs and lavenders or cream with coffee and cappuccino.

- **Autumn:** russet, gold and burnt orange, chocolate and sage green, petrol blue or aqua with cream.

- **Winter:** black, white and silver, blood red with emerald green and gold, aubergine and plum.

Pocket tip 🥂

If you're hiring a lot of equipment for your reception or marquee, remember that plain glassware and classic white china is usually more affordable than coloured varieties and easier to accessorise. Add colour to your tables by using sprinkled petals or metallic glitter instead.

Keeping it green

1. *Use plants as well as cut flowers for decorations, so you can take some home as mementos. If your heart is set on imported flowers, try to ensure they are from Fairtrade growers.*

2. *Include locally-produced foods where you can, even if it is just a cheese or ice-cream from a local dairy farm, a regional beer or a breed of pork or cattle specific to the region. It all cuts down on food miles.*

3. *Choose venues that are either within walking distance of each other or close to public transport stations to cut down the need for lots of cars. If guests do have to drive deep into the countryside, why not hire one bus to ferry them all about?*

4. *Give guests more lasting favours by handing out a packet of seeds for the flowers featured in your decorations or your bouquet, so that they can grow some themselves. You could also decorate the tables with pretty pots of sunflowers which people can take home once the evening is over.*

5. *Buy biodegradable confetti or use petals.*

🌿 FAVOURS 🌿

The tradition of giving favours dates back to the medieval age when unmarried friends would try to grab something lucky of the bride's, maybe her posy or her garter, which they thought would boost their chances of being next down the aisle (rather like an early version of throwing the bride's bouquet). In an attempt to avoid being rugby-tackled by desperate singletons on her big day, some brides started carrying small pieces of coloured ribbon which were known as favours – the same name given to the tokens ladies would give to their favourite knights before a jousting tournament. This meant that there were enough lucky favours to go round.

Traditionally favours were five sugared almonds in a little net bag to represent wealth, health, fertility, happiness and a long life, and were left at each guest's place setting. Whole almonds covered in sugar coating or chocolate are also called dragees and can come individually wrapped in coloured paper.

However, couples are increasingly looking to give their guests something more elaborate and favours are fast becoming mini soaps, bath bombs, mini bottles of liqueur or even fragrances if the budget will allow.

Money saver

If you're having a Saturday wedding and you're budgeting around one pound a person for favours, why not give everyone a lottery ticket and have the DJ reveal the winning numbers once they have been announced on TV?

🐝 ENTERTAINMENT 🐝

Weddings can be a long day if you get married early, but that doesn't mean you have to fill the event with wall-to-wall acts. Guests are perfectly capable of amusing themselves for a while or chatting to others in the lulls between the ceremony, photos, wedding breakfast, speeches and dancing. They have come to celebrate your big day, they haven't booked a package holiday, so you don't have to worry about keeping them entertained from the minute they arrive till the minute they go home.

Pocket tip 🦋

Magicians can help break the ice during a drinks reception or act as a distraction while you go off for photos. Most work better in among guests doing sleight of hand tricks rather than as a full variety-style performance in front of a captive audience. Unless you book a children's magician, that is, in which case having all the little ones seated for a performance involving hats and rabbits can give parents a break.

The wedding industry is full of specialist performers who can do everything from magic tricks, acrobatics, balloon crafting and caricatures, or you can even hire singing waiters, tribute acts and limbo dancers. No wedding needs them all, so the trick is to identify your need and book one good act. And decide who is going to co-ordinate the day once you've booked the venue. Some places have an in-house master of ceremonies who can move proceedings along and make announcements. If not, you can hire them privately, but bear in mind if they have no connection with the venue and its set packages, you will have to make sure you and the venue manager brief him or her properly. It's often easier to brief up the best man to keep things running to time than worrying about it yourself.

Money saver

Thinking of saving some of that nice champagne from the cocktail reception for the speeches and toasts? Think twice. If people have been drinking red and/or white wine with their meal they may not appreciate the expensive labels later in the day. Many wedding planners believe it's best to use the good stuff at the beginning of the reception when people are sober and can appreciate the taste.

🌿 YOUR FIRST DANCE 🌿

The two-left-feet shuffle is on its way out, it seems, as a combination of *Strictly Come Dancing* hysteria and show dances on YouTube has prompted a leap in the number of newlyweds taking dance lessons before their big day. And if you don't fancy the salsa, tango or the foxtrot there's no harm in taking a few waltz lessons so that you can one-two-three without tripping over your own feet, especially as a 2009 poll on www.youandyourwedding.co.uk revealed that the most popular first dance tunes are still dominated by slowies.

The top ten first dance songs from 2009 were:

1. *Wonderful Tonight* by Eric Clapton
2. *Amazed* by Lonestar
3. *Can't Take My Eyes Off You* by Andy Williams
4. *Your Song* by Elton John
5. *Have I Told You Lately* by Rod Stewart

6. *You Do Something To Me* by Paul Weller
7. *Chasing Cars* by Snow Patrol
8. *Fly Me To The Moon* by Frank Sinatra
9. *Greatest Day* by Take That
10. *Stand By Me* by Ben E King

Money saver

Rig your laptop up to the entertainment system or use your iPod to play your own tunes and save on the price of a DJ.

ROSES ARE RED . . .
WEDDING FLOWERS

Roses, lilies, orchids and tulips are the four most popular flowers at a 21st century wedding, usually matched to a colour scheme. Back in the middle ages though, bridal flowers were chosen for more superstitious reasons. Brides often carried posies of herbs and garlic which were thought to keep away the evil spirits on their wedding day, or they included grains such as stalks of corn and barley to represent health and prosperity. Although fragrant herbs like rosemary and lemon grass sometimes find their way into the 21st century bouquet or table centre, most wedding flowers today are chosen for their aesthetic qualities – to suit a theme or a particular colour scheme – rather than because a superstitious bride is worried about demons bringing bad luck. That's not to say though that today's popular bridal flowers don't have their traditional meanings.

FLOWERS AND THEIR
TRADITIONAL MEANINGS

ROSES

Red roses are not just Valentine's Day favourites, they have long been the traditional flower of love, and roses are still the most popular flower for bridal bouquets today. And different coloured roses symbolise different things. White has an obvious meaning – innocence and purity – while pink represents grace and elegance, orange stands for passion and desire, while yellow equals joy and friendship.

Pocket fact 🔗

In the UK lilies are traditionally thought of as funeral flowers, but farther back in time they were associated with fertility and motherhood. The ancient Romans believed lilies sprang from droplets of milk which fell from heaven while the goddess Juno was nursing her baby, Hercules.

OTHER FLOWERS

Other meaningful flowers for weddings include English lavender, which is a symbol of loyalty and devotion, and orange blossom (traditional at Spanish weddings) which represents joy and fulfilment because it flowers and bears fruit at the same time.

Go green

If you're having a church or register office wedding, have a heart for the eco cost of your wedding as well as the budgetary cost and see whether you can make use of the flowers organised by couples marrying before you. When Grace Beesley married Fraser Moores in April 2005, at Windsor's Guildhall they shared the flowers left by the previous bride and groom – HRH Prince Charles and Camilla parker-Bowles – along with cheers and waves from the waiting crowds.

POPULAR WEDDING FLOWERS AND THEIR MEANINGS

Anemone: unfading love
Bird of paradise: fidelity
Gypsophila: everlasting love
Calla lily: beauty ('calla' is Greek for beauty)
Chrysanthemum: cheerfulness and friendship

Daffodil: respect
Dahlia: elegance
Daisy: innocence
Freesia: innocence
Gerbera: innocence
Gladioli: generosity

Hyacinth: playfulness (but not yellow which means jealousy!)
Jasmine: likability
Lily of the valley: sweetness
Narcissus: sweetness

Peony: aphrodisiac
Stephanotis: happiness
Sunflower: loyalty
Tiger lily: wealth
Zinnia: lasting love

The language of flowers

Back in the very proper Victorian age, gentlemen would use the language of flowers to send messages to young ladies who were strictly chaperoned and not easily approached in polite society. If a girl received a posy of roses in bud form it meant her would-be lover was in the first shy and tentative stages of love. If he sent her open flowers in full bloom, on the other hand, her young suitor was said to be bursting with passion!

WHAT DO YOU NEED AND WHERE DO YOU START?

Flowers are traditionally accessories for the main players in your wedding party (bouquets, buttonholes, posies and corsages) and decorations at the ceremony and reception, but they can also leave a big hole in your budget if you're not used to buying them. Flowers, on average, account for between 5%–10% of the budget at a UK wedding, so it's important to find a good florist and spend the money where it will be most appreciated.

Money saver

The flowers you order will be a fixed price per stem or bunch. The florist's time is extra, so the more intricate the arrangement, the bigger the bill. A simple hand-tied posy is quicker and more cost-effective to make than an intricately-wired shower bouquet.

BRIDE'S BOUQUET

Depending on the style of dress and wedding, this can be as subtle as a single stem tied with a discreet ribbon or as elaborate as a cascading bouquet packed with an assortment of flowers, foliage and colours.

Pocket tip

An over arm bouquet (carried on your forearm) of something structural like calla lilies can look striking in photos but it can get quite weighty after a while. Avoid heavy bouquets that will mean you have to keep swapping arms. You'll need your other hand free to hold your dad's arm, your groom's hand and your champagne glass!

BUTTONHOLES

Providing buttonholes for every guest is expensive and not necessary. Generally speaking you order a buttonhole for the groom, his best man/men, immediate male family members such as fathers, grandfathers, brothers, brother-in-law and sons, your ushers and any friends giving a reading or a recital.

If you're trying to keep costs down, stick to one simple flower which a florist can prepare reasonably quickly, rather than a confection of flower heads and foliage. If you're ordering a lot of buttonholes, choose a flower like the carnation which is quite hardwearing so that they can be made up the night before and still look fresh. Colour-wise the groom often wears a different colour buttonhole to the rest of his party so that he stands out; normally people pick out a colour in the bride's bouquet for the groom while the rest of the men wear a colour reflecting the bridesmaids' bouquets.

Pocket tip

Buttonholes are usually delivered to the ceremony venue all together and are pinned on as everyone arrives.

CORSAGES

Traditionally both mums are given a special flower arrangement to highlight their importance in the proceedings, but it's a good idea to check with them first if they want to wear one. Unlike men's suits which are reasonably robust, mums often choose silks or crepe for their son or daughter's big day and these can rip easily with pins and weighty corsages. Ask if they would prefer to wear a wrist corsage instead. Generally speaking a mum's corsage is slightly more ornate than a buttonhole and popular flowers include: roses, lily of the valley, orchids, gerberas, freesias, lilies, heathers and alstromeria and foliage is usually ivy, wax flowers, eucalyptus and bear grass.

Pocket tip 🎀

Buttonholes are traditionally worn on the left lapel of a suit (just above the heart, according to custom), while the mothers of the bride and groom traditionally wear their corsages on the right side of their dress or jacket, or higher towards the shoulder.

BOUQUETS OR POSIES FOR BRIDESMAIDS

Adult bridesmaids usually carry flowers that mirror the bride's bouquet either in different shades or tones, or as smaller versions. For young flower girls, popular options include a posy on a ribbon or a little basket of flowers or petals.

Money saver

Stick to just one or two types of flowers in the same colour and give your bouquet a 'wow' feel for less budget. Roses and gerberas or roses and anemones work well together, especially accented with some hypericum berries for a winter wedding.

🌾 DECORATIONS FOR THE 🌸 CEREMONY VENUE

CHURCH FLOWERS

If you're having a religious ceremony, remember you're only in the venue for a short time compared to the amount of time your guests spend at the reception, so split the budget accordingly. In popular months you might find there are at least two weddings per day, so you could approach the other couple and see if you can agree on sharing flowers and splitting the cost. Some churches also have parishioners whose job it is to do the flowers. To avoid a big shock on the day make a point of meeting up beforehand. Someone who has been doing the church flowers for 40 years might not share your more modern vision of wedding flowers!

Money saver

Ask your florist about church flowers that can double up for use at the reception. The key here is to make them portable. Pew ends can often be transported to the second venue to decorate the top table providing they are not too intricately wired. Pedestal arrangements at the front of the church could look just as effective in the foyer of your reception venue, providing someone can fit them in their car without crushing them. Or maybe your florist will transport them for you?

CIVIL CEREMONY

It's unlikely you'll need floral decorations in a register office as the ceremony itself is very quick, space is limited and there is usually a standard simple floral arrangement already in place. At a licensed venue where you can also hold a celebration afterwards, however, there is far more scope to create flower decorations that can be moved quickly from the room where you take your vows to the drinks reception room.

Pocket tip 🥂

Lots of small flower arrangements don't have as much impact as a couple of elaborate ones but they will cost you at least as much — if not more — as you're paying for the florist's time. Put arrangements where people will see them, ie on or behind the top table and beside the cake table. Don't bother spending fortunes decorating the door of the venue. People only see it once when they arrive.

TABLE DECORATIONS

Although large elaborate centrepieces create a real wow factor when your guests enter the dining hall, once they're sitting down they can actually get in the way of conversation, so keep centrepieces high or low enough for people to talk over or under. A few flowers beautifully arranged around chunky cathedral candles can look just as effective as a big display.

Money saver

Bulk out more expensive blooms with value-for-money fillers such as gypsophila, or make simple but effective table arrangements from carnations — often overlooked as a cheap garage-forecourt option but deceptively effective.

UNIQUE WAYS TO DECORATE A VENUE WITH FLOWERS

Alternative containers

Classic white roses arranged in giant martini glasses look very 'Moulin Rouge' for a chic city celebration, and dainty flowers like sweet peas or lilac in vintage mugs and jugs give a lovely country fete feel.

Fruity accessories

Large glass bowls stacked with dramatically coloured citrus fruits look vibrant as centrepieces, especially if simply accented with lemon and white petals scattered at the bottom of the bowl and around the table.

Fish bowls

These have been popular for a while and look effective with structured flowers like calla lilies inside. To add texture and avoid the bowl looking empty, twirl some grasses inside the bowl first.

Mirrored vases

Fill with ice-white flowers and frost with glitter to make lovely winter wonderland decorations.

Cake stands

Who says they have to feature cakes. Vintage style cake stands covered with pastel and coffee-coloured roses in little jugs and pots give any table a stylish retro feel.

Bulbs and herbs

For a more rustic feel to your table, arrange groups of different shaped pots featuring fragrant herbs (thyme, rosemary, lemon grass) or flowering bulbs like hyacinths on the tables.

Water features

If your venue has a pond or a fountain, ask if you can float gerbera flower heads on top of the water.

Go green

If you hate the thought of your beautiful centrepieces dying after a few days, use potted plants such as orchids, hydrangea – or even little pots of fragrant herbs such as rosemary – and give them to guests afterwards as thank you gifts or favours. Phalaenopsis orchids are good for this as they flower all year. You can use cymbidium orchids too, although they only flower in winter and spring.

🌿 SEASONAL FLOWERS 🌸

Many flowers are available in more than one season, but to keep your wedding fresh and seasonal (and help keep your budget in check) these are some tried-and-tested wedding favourites:

- **Spring:** daffodils, tulips, freesia, peony, amaryllis, ranunculus, chincherinchee, anemone, mimosa, phlox, sweet pea, lilac and lily of the valley (generally quite expensive).

- **Summer:** rose, sweet pea, magnolia, peonies, lavender, lily, bouvardia, marigold, freesia, gerbera, sunflower, chrysanthemum and hydrangea (big and blousy with papers leaves, a single head in a square mirrored cube makes a simple but cost-effective centrepiece).

- **Autumn:** gerbera, hydrangea, gladioli, bouvardia, delphinium, celosia, cornflower, dahlia, gladiolus, lavender, nerine, phlox and scabious (sounds horrid but the purple/blue flowers look beautiful in bouquets).

- **Winter:** snowdrop, nerine, iris, hyacinth, camellia, lilac, anemone, bouvardia, hypericum berries, mimosa, marigold, stephanotis, bird of paradise, delphinium, amaryllis aster, gypsophila, lilac and ranunculus.

Pocket fact 🕭

The tulip season is October/November to April/May so for winter and spring weddings, tulips are really good value, but at both ends of the season the price increases dramatically. In summer tulips have to be flown in from the southern hemisphere which can quadruple their price.

NATIONAL FLOWERS

If you come from different cultures, why not choose flower arrangements that reflect your different cultures? National flowers that are great for weddings include:

- England: rose
- Scotland: thistle or heather
- Wales: daffodil
- Singapore: cymbidium orchid
- Malaysia: hibiscus

- Pakistan: jasmine
- India: lotus
- Bangladesh: white water lily
- South Africa: protea
- Italy: poppy or white lily

- Greece: Guernsey lily
- France: lily
- Poland: cornflower
- Turkey: tulip

🌸 FIVE STEPS TO FINDING 🌸 THE RIGHT FLORIST

1. Recommendations from friends and family are best, but make sure it's because they've used that particular florist for a wedding or a party, and not just because they buy flowers from the shop on the way home from work!

2. Your venue may recommend someone they like to work with. On the plus side it means the florist is familiar with the space you've chosen for your celebration, but it may also be based on a mutual business arrangement – or even the old pals act – so make sure it's the best value for you.

3. Be on the lookout for flowers everywhere you go – in restaurants, shops or even office foyers. If you see something you like, ask who arranged them.

4. Do a recce around flower markets to get an idea of pricing and to see which flowers jump out at you. It means you can approach your florist with a better idea of what you want.

5. Set yourselves a realistic budget. A good florist will help you choose the right flowers and arrangements within that budget. If they're more intent on getting you to spend more than you'd like, find someone else!

Pocket tip 🌿

If someone in the main bridal party (bride, groom, best man, father of the bride) suffers from hay fever, avoid flowers with lots of scent such as hyacinths, lisianthus or narcissus which can cause problems. Stick to roses, anemones, tulips or ranunculus.

DOING THE FLOWERS YOURSELF

Taking on all the flowers of a wedding can be quite a challenge to a novice, so consider doing just part of the day, ie the bridesmaids' posies or the flowers in the church rather than the whole lot!

Pocket fact

Most cut roses are bred with fewer thorns and any that do remain can usually be removed with a small knife. However, this is a job best left to the professionals, so if you're thinking of arranging flowers yourself — maybe for the church or ceremony venue — ask your florist to remove any thorns before you take them home.

Flower astrology

Still stumped over which flowers to choose for your wedding? Maybe it's written in the stars . . .

Fire signs (Aries, Leo, Sagittarius)
Related colours: red, orange, gold, yellow, deep blue and purple
Consider: tulips, red roses, amaryllis, marigold, sunflower, lisianthus, carnation

Earth signs (Taurus, Virgo, Capricorn)
Related colours: pastel pink and blue, purple, blue and brown, grey and sage green
Consider: lavender, sweet pea, lilac, violet, thistle, African violet, jasmine

Air signs (Libra, Gemini, Aquarius)
Related colours: yellow, green, turquoise
Consider: ranunculus, mimosa, daffodil, cymbidium orchid, freesia, arum lily, bird of paradise

Water signs (Cancer, Scorpio, Pisces)
Related colours: silver and metallic blue, maroon, purple-red, grey green, cream
Consider: red hot poker, peony, iris, delphinium, cornflower, jasmine, lilac, gypsophila

SAY CHEESE!
PHOTOGRAPHY

Wedding photography has come a long way from the days when couples 'watched the birdie' in the late Victorian and Edwardian era. No-one smiled in these wedding pics, in fact they all looked distinctly formal and cheesed off in the stiff non-smiling sittings that were colour touched afterwards so that everyone had unnaturally pink cheeks and blue eyes. Today the trend in wedding photos has moved away from formal line ups, to a mix of family groups and what is known as 'reportage photography'.

Pocket fact &

Bad photography is number one in the biggest disappointments among couples after the wedding. Not because it happens the most often, but because it is the lasting memory of the day and the one disaster couples find out about after the event. If something goes wrong on the day (the bell ringers fail to turn up or the soup is cold) it soon tends to get forgotten in the excitement of the celebration. (To deal with unforeseen hiccups see Wedding Insurance, pages 54–55).

REPORTAGE PHOTOGRAPHY

The dictionary definition of reportage is 'the act or process of reporting an event' and many photographers offer a more relaxed, fly-on-the-wall style of photography but you need to be sure this is actually want you want.

PROS

- Reportage style captures snapshots of the day you would otherwise miss, such as flower girls spinning around in their big skirts, guests throwing their heads back laughing, or the bride and groom sharing a private kiss.

- It tells the story of the day, capturing different locations within your venue rather than having lots of line-ups in the same place.

CONS

- Without a pre-agreed shot list, there's no guarantee that the photographer will get in all the key players. Imagine the family fallout if the photos come back without a picture of your mum or your nan!

- Reportage storytelling is not going to look like a fashion shoot, which is what many brides mistake it for. Beautiful fashion shots in a bridal magazine take hours to set up with stylists and models and are often just as posed as the formal family line-ups.

🐝 PLANNING YOUR SHOT LIST 🐝

Professional photographers generally agree the best compromise is a set of pre-agreed family shots, mixed in with a few more candid, fly-on-the-wall approach. A lot of companies now work in pairs, so while one is taking a picture of the bride's family, the other is capturing shots of the guests milling around at the drinks reception, although hiring two photographers rather than one is obviously going to bump up your costs.

Here is an example of a typical shot list:

- Bride getting ready at home, often informal
- Bride with parents and/or siblings
- Bride leaving for ceremony/getting into car
- Groom and best man arriving at ceremony
- Bride's arrival

- Groom waiting at altar
- Bride and father/groom walking down the aisle or approaching the celebrant
- Reciting vows (if allowed)
- Exchanging rings (if allowed)
- Signing the register
- Walking back down the aisle
- Couple shot full-length
- Couple shot close-up
- With best man and attendants
- With groom's family
- With bride's family
- With everyone
- Cutting the cake
- The toasts and speeches

Pocket tip 🥂

Most ministers welcome photographers inside church but there can be certain restrictions, eg the photographer may not be allowed to step beyond a certain point at the front of the church or there may be a ban on photos during the vows or prayers. Make sure you check and tell your photographer exactly what they can/cannot do.

💐 QUESTIONS TO ASK BEFORE BOOKING A PHOTOGRAPHER 💐

Q: What packages do you offer?

Ask if travel expenses are included and get a good estimate of what they might be. Some photographers only work up until the wedding breakfast and charge more to cover the evening entertainment, so check how long you are booking them for. Also ask if there are any prints included in the package, or if you get a disk with all the pictures, etc.

Q: Were the examples we're looking at taken by the actual photographer coming on the day?

Is there a chance the studio will subcontract your job to an associate or a freelancer whose work you haven't seen? If so, you want to be looking at their work, not a promotional album that could have been taken by anyone.

Pocket tip

Find someone you gel with immediately. You'll be working with this person for a few very pressured but precious hours, so make sure you like each other. Also don't automatically assume someone who boasts 40 years experience is going to be better than a younger photographer. Make sure their work has moved with the times.

Q: Are the photos we're looking at all taken from the same wedding?

Anyone can take a few good pics; the benchmark of a good photographer is an album that shows a consistent high standard from Here Comes the Bride to the final waltz. A selection of 'best bits' from lots of weddings doesn't give you a true picture of someone's abilities.

Q: Do you know our venue already or are you prepared to visit it to check out the location?

Half an hour looking around a venue together before the big day can really pay off. It can save a lot of time on the day and gives you and the photographer a chance to think about where to take pictures if the weather plays up.

Pocket fact

It may be your wedding but your photographer automatically owns copyright to your photos. This is so that they can make additional income when your friends and family order pictures. Some photographers will sell copyright to the couple for an additional fee, so it's worth asking the question.

🐝 WHAT A POSER: TIPS ON 🐝 GETTING TIMELESS PHOTOS

Models and actresses don't look great in photos by accident. They know a few camera tricks that play up their good points and mask any bad ones. A few hours practising these moves in front of the mirror could pay off in the wedding album.

- **Don't** stand square on to the camera. It can add as much as half a stone (around three kilos) because your shoulders are about three times as wide as your head.

- **Do** turn 30–40 degrees to the side, enough for the shoulders to come down to just twice the width of the head.

- **Do** smile with your eyes. Laughing is the best way to get natural smiles so encourage friends and family to lark about or shout out one-liners while you're posing for photos.

- **Don't** hold a smile too long. A-listers on the red carpet know to smile at the last moment before the camera clicks, even to the point of moving the head slightly away and then back into shot.

- **Do** put your weight on the foot farthest away from the camera and dip the shoulder away too (things become smaller the farther away they get). By dipping your shoulders, you also tip your pelvis which makes a flattering S shape through the shoulders, waist and pelvis.

- **Do** make sure your groom, best man and ushers don't pose with their hands in front of their trousers like footballers waiting for a free kick. Nothing makes a man look more self-conscious!

Pocket fact 🐝

If the bride's high heels mean she is as tall, or even taller, than her groom, photographers often suggest taking pictures on steps, with the bride standing on a step below her groom, to adjust the height difference. When Mickey Rooney married fellow screen star Ava Gardner in 1941, a stool had to be brought in so that the pocket-sized actor could be brought up to the height of the statuesque screen idol for the pictures.

🎬 VIDEOGRAPHY 🎬

Don't be fooled by people who tell you they have state-of-the-art equipment, the sort they use on TV/films. So what? If the person can't use it properly, it doesn't matter a jot how hi-tech it is.

There are a few different styles of wedding video to choose from. Your options include:

- **Story telling style**: more traditional style which tells the story of the day.

- **Documentary style**: less chronological and doesn't try to cover every stage of the day but gives a flavour.

- **Interview style**: more interactive, and has the couple and key players talking to camera and even sending their good wishes.

Pocket tip 🥂

Most filmmakers will have a stock of music soundtracks that they have copyright usage for. If you have a particular piece of music you really want to use, it may cost extra for them to source the copyright.

ALL THE LITTLE DETAILS: OTHER THINGS YOU NEED TO PLAN

GIFT LISTS

Back in 1972, when the number of weddings in the UK peaked at 480,285, the most popular wedding gifts were avocado dishes, fondues and hostess trolleys. In the days before online gift lists, the happy couple got what they were given, kept schtum about the five lava lamps and buried unwanted shag rugs in the attic. Today's newlyweds are far less accepting. A study by amazon.co.uk revealed over a third of Scottish couples flogged their unwanted wedding gifts at boot sales and one in four was disappointed with a third of their presents.

HOW TO SET UP A GIFT LIST

There are a number of ways to help your guests pick the right present for you: via a specialist wedding gift company, through a gift list service at a high street chain or department store or via a specific company/ies (such as Spode or Wedgwood), if you're happy to restrict your gifts to one particular field or manufacturer. Each gift list is set up slightly differently, but if you were to register with a well-known department store, for instance, it would probably work like this.

- You and your fiancé register a set number of weeks before the wedding. Most gift list providers recommend not too far ahead as stock changes all the time.

- You compile your master list, usually by walking around the store with a scanner and literally scanning everything that takes your fancy.

- Your gift list goes live around the time your invitations are sent, along with details of the gift list; reference number etc, and guests can then usually buy online, in store or over the phone.

- The list updates itself all the time, telling you who has bought what. Most have a facility for guests to leave messages, and you usually have the option to add more things as you go if there is a bit of a run on a certain price range.

Rule of thumb 🎂

It may tempting to stick to lots of thing around a modest 25–35 pound mark, but don't feel embarrassed about putting a couple of higher-price items on your list. Groups of mates at work or at your football or golf club will often get together to buy you something more substantial.

According to amazon.co.uk the 'top 3 most-wanted' wedding gifts are:

1. Flat screen TV
2. Gift vouchers
3. His & hers iPod/DAB radio

Technology isn't the only popular choice for gift lists though; according to John Lewis, there's been such a jump in the number of couples asking friends and family for camping equipment on their wedding gift list that the requests for sleeping bags have gone up by 88%!

Pocket tip 🥂

If you're hoping to reap the benefits of a well-planned gift list, be sure to invite all your aged aunts and uncles. A survey by www.greenbee.com in 2008 found that people aged over 65 are the most generous. They are willing to spend over £63 per wedding gift, compared to an average spend of £48 per person for those under 65.

UNUSUAL GIFT LISTS

- Guests at the wedding of Elizabeth Hurley and Arun Nayar were invited to donate animals (such as a Gloucester Old Spot pig, costing £189) for their farm.

- To celebrate his marriage to wife Laura, former Goodie Bill Oddie asked guests to bring garden gnomes as wedding presents, a collection of which still stand in the grounds of his home.

- What do you want, blood? Yes actually! Regular blood donors Daniel and Jane Cliff from Oxfordshire decided to do away with the traditional gift list when they were married in the summer of 2009 and asked guests to donate some blood instead. At least 25 of them agreed to submit to the needle for a good cause!

- Susan Brown, the registrar who married Madonna and Guy Ritchie, presented the newlyweds with a gift of two toilet rolls, claiming they were long, strong and representative of a happy marriage. (Hmmm!)

Pocket fact ✍

In the Jewish tradition, it's bad luck to receive knives as a wedding gift. In case someone should give knives, the bride should transform the exchange into a financial transaction by giving a penny or nominal sum for the knives.

🌿 BIG DAY TRANSPORT 🌿

Daisy, Daisy give me your answer do... Daisy might have been happy on a bicycle made for two, but most brides want to arrive at their wedding in style, so unless you have friends with a smart white Rolls-Royce, you're probably going to need to hire something.

Pocket fact &

A vintage 1934 Austin Healey called Gertrude took three gener-ations of blushing brides from the same family to church over a period of nearly 60 years. In 2005 Fru Grace followed in the same tyre tracks as her mother (Sheila, in 1969) and grandmother (Joan, in 1946) in the family car after her dad and brother scoured the country for six months for parts to get it through the MOT.

There are a few basic rules to bear in mind when looking for your perfect mode of transport:

1. Soft tops are very chic but play havoc with your hair. Don't go for the Chitty Chitty Bang Bang idea unlesss you're happy to take your chances with the elements.

2. If you're hiring a specialist car and driver, bear in mind the location of the supplier, as you will be charged mileage and petrol on top of the booking costs to get there and back. If your wedding is in London, it will be expensive to bring in a specialist car from Wales for example, so try to find something closer by.

3. Think logistically if you fancy a low, sporting model, especially if you are going for a full skirt or long veil. Getting in and out of the car will not be easy.

4. Some car hire firms put flowers on the back shelf. If you would prefer they didn't, say so.

5. If you have a really stylish car that would make a good backdrop for pictures, set aside some time with your photographer and ask the driver not to rush off. Make sure

there is a suitable location though. Car parks are not the most attractive places for wedding photos.

Pocket fact &

Who says the A-list travel everywhere first class? After his wedding Take That's Mark Owen whisked his new wife to their honeymoon suite in a vintage Volkswagen camper van decked out with rose petals on the floor and a love heart shaped out of twigs.

Pocket Tip 🔔

Check the car you have hired is regularly used for weddings and there's nothing inside that can catch, snag or stain your dress. When Maria Wright of Bristol emerged blushing from the limousine hired to take her to her wedding, she discovered that the August heat wave had caused the cherry red interior to 'bleed' colour all over her expensive dress.

🌿 STAG AND HEN PARTIES 🌿

Once a fairly low-key pub crawl or meal out, hen and stag parties began to snowball into weekends and then week-long trips abroad until the 2008 credit crunch finally began to curb the excesses.

Even so, the stag or hen party is often the biggest expense for friends and family. Research by financial institutions suggests that the average Brit spends anything from £350–£400 on a friend's wedding (and as many as one in seven of those are not happy about it!). Around a third of this cost is thought to go on the hen or stag do, followed by gifts for the couple, outfits and travelling costs. And spare a thought for the best man, whose job it is to organise the stag party. Another banking survey found that it could cost him as much as £530 for the privilege – nearly £200 more than it is likely to cost his opposite number on the girls' side – the chief bridesmaid.

Pocket tip

The insurance industry estimates around one in five stags lose their wallet, phone, iPod or other valuables during their jollies so it's a good idea for the best man to make sure everyone is insured.

Traditional stag/hen elements:

- Silly costumes
- Games
- Embarrassing stories about the stag/hen
- Lots of booze
- A stripper

WHAT'S THE ALTERNATIVE?

For the groom

Not every groom (or even bride!) wants to get wasted on his stag night and arrive home with an embarrassing tattoo. Two thirds of grooms and best men interviewed in 2009 said they would prefer a more adventurous, adrenaline-boosting stag experience to the traditional boozy stag weekend (although whether they were surveyed with their brides-to-be in earshot and were simply being careful with their answer was not established!). Top activity from the survey was paintballing (22%) followed by rock and mountain climbing (13%).

Pocket fact

In the first half of the noughties, the most popular stag destinations were Ireland, Amsterdam, Spain, France and Prague in the Czech Republic. But as the decade went on, emerging Eastern European markets started to make their mark, with cities like Tallinn, Riga, Bratislava, Sofia and Budapest now competing for the stag pound.

For the bride

Like her man, not every bride wants to trip through Brighton town centre on a pub crawl wearing L-plates.

Here are a few ideas for an alternative hen party (just search the internet for suppliers in your area):

Top ten alternative hen nights

1. Pamper hen day.,Many spas now create special packages with treatments and champagne for a bride and her hens.

2. Swan parties. Similar to above, involving an afternoon champagne tea so that mum, aunties and other older family members can join in too.

3. Hat-making courses. Many milliners are now offering afternoon or full-day hat-making courses where your hens can make their own wedding hats over a couple of glasses of wine.

4. Cookery courses. As above but the idea is you get to sit down and enjoy the meal you've slaved over.

5. Wine tasting. Well, we're back to the wine again but at least you learn something.

6. Activity courses. Who says getting muddy is only for the boys? An increase in away-day activities means hens are also dong everything from abseiling to kayaking.

7. Cutting a record. This is the next stage on from karaoke, you buy some studio time and record a song together which the best man can play during his speech. Should bring the house down!

8. Dancing lessons. *Strictly Corne Dancing* has brought out the ballroom diva in many a bride and dance clubs across the country are offering bespoke dancing sessions that could make perfect hen dos. A more extreme version of this are pole dancing classes: perhaps not one to take your granny on!

9. Silver screen day. Hire a cinema and have your own private screening of your favourite girly movies.

10. Stay in. In a right royal way, though. Order your favourite take-aways, get everyone to bring a bottle and a beauty treat (face pack, foot massager, nail kit) and watch girly films. (See our pick of wedding-themed films on pages 28–32.)

Pocket fact

Traditionally, the groom goes somewhere blokey with his stags while the bride hits the spa or the wine bar with her hens, but a trend has grown up in recent years for both parties to meet up somewhere neutral at the end of the same night to compare notes, known as STEN or HAG parties.

🌿 GIFTS FOR YOUR HELPERS 🌿

It's touching to say 'thank you' to mum, dad, sisters, bridesmaids and the best man with gifts, often presented during the speeches. Traditionally mums got bouquets, the best man got whisky or cufflinks (these may be better presented before the day so he can wear them for the wedding) and the bridesmaids were given jewellery, such as earrings or a bangle. With a large wedding though this can prove costly, so it pays to think personal rather than pounds.

Money saver

Why not dig out an old forgotten photo of you with your bridesmaid/best man at Brownie camp or in a rugby team line-up and have it framed. A treasured memory's worth a dozen bottles of perfume.

🌿 EXCESS ALL AREAS – THE 🌿 CELEBRITY WEDDING

If anyone knows how to go over the top at a wedding, it's the celebrities that grace the papers and magazines across the world. Here are just a few examples of celebs taking their nuptials to the extreme:

- Kylie Minogue is thought to have earned a six-figure sum for an appearance at the six-day wedding celebrations of Vanisha Mittal, daughter of steel magnate Lakshmi in 2004. The proud father also hired private jets to fly in hundreds of guests to Paris and spent an estimated £30m, making it a contender for the most expensive wedding ever.

- Donald Trump reportedly spent half a million dollars on flowers ($10,000 alone just to have them flown from New York) when he married Melania Klaus in Palm Beach Florida. Even the five-foot cake was decorated with 3,000 blooms.

- Business tycoon Peter Shalson spent an estimated £5m on his celebrations (he made his fortune out of plastic coat hangers) when he married bride Pauline in 2007. Much of the cost went on his entertainment. Elton John performed four songs, including *Your Song* and *Can You Feel the Love Tonight* (where he was joined by the West End cast of *The Lion King*), and a set by Kool & the Gang got the party started.

- In 2004 US society girl Tori Spelling's (daughter of *Dynasty* and *Beverly Hills 90210* tycoon Aaron) wedding cost daddy a cool $1m which Forbes.com worked out to equal $71,000 dollars for each month of her short-lived marriage to actor Charlie Shanian.

- Wayne and Coleen Rooney spent an estimated £5m on their wedding in Italy. Yet they only had 65 guests – which puts the price-per-head at over £75,000!

THE BRIDAL PARTY

The smoothest, most memorable and most enjoyable weddings are those where everyone knows the role they have to play, so invest a bit of time putting together a brief for the key players, preferably a few weeks or months before the wedding, not the night before!

❧ THE BRIDE ❧

Being a bride today can be a full-time occupation and the term 'bridezilla' has come to encapsulate all that is extreme about the trials and tribulations of planning a wedding. Entire TV channels are devoted to the marriage industry, wedding shows across the UK get tens of thousands of visitors a year and bridal chatrooms are buzzing with advice and ideas. Unlike the days when brides were chattels to be used for financial gain between families, brides are now most definitely in the driving seat and upping the revs when it comes to wedding planning.

Pocket fact ✑

The term 'bride' is thought to come from the days when knights called their intended their 'bride' in honour of St Bridget, the patron saint of healers in Ireland. Bridget should also be called the patron saint of impatient girlfriends as it's said she also introduced the tradition of leap year proposals (see p.3).

BRIDE'S DUTIES

A bride has few specific duties on the day, other than to make a big entrance and look beautiful. However, she is involved in just about every decision in the run up to the day, unlike the groom who often has no idea what the bride or the bridesmaids are going to look like and only a rudimentary grasp of the floral decorations. One of the main things a bride has to do is to appoint a chief bridesmaid or matron of honour to be her right hand and rally round the other bridesmaids, flower girls or pages, who are also her choices.

Pocket fact

A bride traditionally wears something old (to maintain links with her family and her past), something new (representing her hopes for the future), something borrowed (preferably from a happily married sister or friend) and something blue (historically blue stood for purity and virginity and a blue wedding dress was considered lucky right up until the 1800s).

Just remember, while it can be easy to get caught up in all the planning and worry yourself sick over centrepieces and favours, this is your day so take time to breathe and enjoy yourself. All those 1,001 little things you were worrying about will pale into insignificance on the day itself. Just have fun!

Stress buster

Sprinkle your pillow the night before with one or two drops of calming oils such as neroli or orange blossom to help you get some much needed shut eye!

🌿 THE GROOM 🌿

The modern groom is a far more passive creature than his ancient cousin. The Anglo-Saxon groom would target his intended from afar, kidnap her and whisk her off into hiding (often against her will) with the help of his trusty wing man (the prototype of the best man). He would then keep her holed up for a month till her family gave up looking or she was expecting a child – whichever came first.

Today a groom's duties are rather more civilised and he is far more likely to be at menu tastings, venue open days and wedding shows with his bride to be. In fact, in the spirit of equality, 'bridezilla' has now been joined by the 'groomzilla' and brides are finding their rugby-playing, beer-swilling boyfriends suddenly stressing about the colour of the napkin rings and whether to have a rose or a gerbera in his buttonhole.

> *Pocket fact* &
>
> *The groom traditionally stands on the right of the bride during the ceremony in order to keep his sword arm free. In the days when brides were often kidnapped by an ambitious suitor, it helped if a groom could fend off her would-be rescuers with his right hand and hang on to his prize with his left.*

GROOM'S DUTIES

Beyond choosing a best man, writing a moving speech and having a stag night, the groom traditionally paid for (or at least took responsibility) for:

- His outfits and the outfits for his groom's party and ushers

- The engagement and wedding rings

- The marriage licence fee and any costs for the ceremony such as choir, bell ringers or registrar's fee

- Transport to the ceremony for himself and his best man

- Transport to the first night hotel and the hotel itself if it's different to the reception venue (this is also a good job to delegate to the best man)

- Gifts for the best man and ushers

Pocket fact &

At the traditional Saturday wedding, grooms have been known to update guests about the half-time scores of football matches during the speeches — usually to the assembled groans of the females — but groom Graham Fletcher went one step further. In 2006, less than an hour after he had said 'till death us do part', he and six of his party dashed to the nearest pub to watch England vs Paraguay in the World Cup, leaving bride Shelly to mingle with guests in Brixham, Devon.

MOTHER-OF-THE-BRIDE

Adam was the luckiest man; he had no mother-in-law
Mark Twain, American writer (1835–1910)

The butt of so many mother-in-law jokes during the speeches, the role of mother of the bride has a certain cachet. Because the bride's father traditionally escorts his daughter to the wedding separately, the MOB is the penultimate person to arrive (usually escorted by the best man, her son or the head usher so she doesn't have to enter the ceremony alone). It means she gets to make a bit of an entrance, so that everyone gets to see her hat and she can do a little regal waving from the front pew before the bride arrives.

Pocket fact &

Formal etiquette used to dictate that female guests should keep on their hats until the mother of the bride removed hers. This was sometimes at the start of the reception, sometimes not till the end of the meal. However, the tradition has fallen out of use in recent years, partly because no one really knows about the custom anyway and partly because it's not so practical with the fashion for hair accessories and fascinators that are part of the hairstyle itself.

MOB'S DUTIES

Aside from finding the perfect hat the mother of the bride's duties include:

- Supporting her little girl in all the planning and trying to avoid phrases like 'that's not how we did it . . .' and 'if you ask me. . .'
- Helping the couple draw up a list (and prune if necessary) of family members who are possible invitees
- Getting involved in setting the budget and keeping a track of deposits and bookings
- Helping pick out the stationery and agreeing the wording, depending on who is hosting the day
- Checking with the groom's mum that she is not wearing the same colour outfit as her – social suicide!

Pocket fact

One proud mother was so keen for her daughter to get married on time, she used her position as a city councillor in York to test a new traffic system. Ann Reid had all the traffic lights set to green, partly, she claimed, to test the system and partly so that daughter Hannah's convoy to the ceremony didn't get held up. She later apologised for her lack of judgement!

FATHER OF THE BRIDE

Once upon a time, the FOB was the long-suffering individual who paid for everything but had a say over very little. (Think Spencer Tracy or Steve Martin in the movies of the same name!) To the relief of most modern-day FOBs, less than 10% of weddings are now funded by the bride's family alone.

FOB'S DUTIES

- Make it clear up front what – if any – financial help is available towards the wedding

- Arrange a get together with the groom's family to try to maintain harmony throughout the run-up to the wedding

- Go to any fittings required to hire formal wear, waistcoats, cravats etc

- Offer to escort his daughter down the aisle to say her vows

- Tell the bride she looks more beautiful than he has ever seen her without being sentimental and making her mascara run

- Make the first speech at the reception to welcome guests and toast the happy couple

- Join the bride and groom on the dance floor after their first dance with the bride's mother

🐝 MOTHER AND FATHER 🐝 OF THE GROOM

Sometimes overlooked in the nuptial hierarchy, the MOG and FOG are like ministers without portfolio. That's to say they are really key people in the proceedings but they don't traditionally have a fixed role. While the bride's mum often goes to dress fittings and on shopping expeditions, it's not so likely for the groom's mum to be invited, although it's not unknown. The groom's dad doesn't traditionally give a speech either, although that's not always the case now, as more and more couples are embracing a philosophy whereby anyone can speak if they have something to say!

Pocket tip 🥂

If the father of the groom wants to say a few words too, it's a nice idea to do it between the bride's dad (speaker 1) and the groom (speaker 2) rather than wait till everyone else has finished. Traditionally the best man speaks last, closing his speech with a few words on how the celebrations are going to proceed.

WAYS TO INVOLVE YOUR FOG AND MOG

- MOG: go dress shopping, opinion on flowers, help cutting down guest list and rounding up RSVPS

- FOG: help with the stag night, check formal wear fits, make a small speech after the FOB.

 BRIDESMAIDS

Traditionally, the role of the bridesmaid was two-fold: it was both to 'serve' the bride as a maid on her special day, but also to act as a buffer against evil spirits and to keep the bride pure and pro-tected. Obviously, the more times a maid fought back against these evil spirits, the less pure she became, hence the phrase 'three times the bridesmaid, never the bride!' Although there is also a belief that if she acted as a bridesmaid seven times – seven being a lucky number – she would come full circle and wipe the slate clean.

Pocket tip

61% of today's bridesmaids are the bride's best friend. And that includes male best friends, otherwise known as 'bridesmen'. Usually her childhood friend, a 'bridesman's' role is to be at the end of the phone with a sympathetic ear and to help the bride get organised on the big day. And if he can't help her adjust her bridal underwear at least he can pour the champagne. A 'brides-man' usually wears a suit in the same shade as the groom but with accessories (shirt, waistcoat, tie) to match the bridesmaids.

BRIDESMAIDS' DUTIES

- Helping the bride get ready

- Either lead or follow the bride down the aisle, depending on the style of ceremony

- Stand at the altar

- Look after the bride's bouquet during the ceremony

- Help usher guests at the reception and make sure everyone is having fun

CHIEF BRIDESMAID

While a bride can choose any number of bridesmaids she usually nominates a chief bridesmaid, or maid of honour, to be her right hand 'man' during the planning, to help out during the ceremony and reception and to keep the other bridesmaids in order.

CHIEF BRIDESMAID'S DUTIES

- Being supportive is top of the list, listening patiently while the bride dithers over decisions, complains about meddling family, and flies into bridezilla rages

- Shopping with the bride for dress and accessories; coming to some agreement among the other bridesmaids over what colours and styles to wear that also keeps the bride happy

- Arranging (or at least assist in organising) the hen night

- Attending the rehearsal for the ceremony

- Staying with the bride the night before the wedding

- Helping the bride get ready on the big day

- Arranging for a little bag of touch-up make-up to be on hand for the photos

- Taking the bride's flowers during the ceremony

- Walking back down the aisle beside the best man

- Posing for photos

- Dancing with the best man during the couple's first dance

- Giving a short chief bridesmaid's speech (increasingly common but optional)

- Helping the bride change from day to evening look (ie removing the veil or changing to a cocktail dress)

- Making sure the bride has her overnight bag in the right place for her first night; arranging to have the dress cleaned as soon as possible while the newlyweds are on honeymoon (this is often also a mother-of-the-bride job)

Pocket fact &

The average number of bridesmaids is three, although bride-to-be Michelle O'Reilly from Derby was in such a dither over who to choose that she asked all 24 people on her shortlist to walk down the aisle with her! But even that's nowhere near the world record — that currently stands at a staggering 79 bridesmaids, set in Ontario, Canada in 2003 by Suresh Joachim!

🌸 BEST MAN 🌸

Traditionally this is the groom's supportive right hand man, a 007-figure who gets him (and the rings) to the church on time, sorts out difficult situations (late-running florists, broken down cars, drunken guests) and sweeps the elderly aunties off their feet on the dance floor. Realistically, the minute you appoint a best man, he spends the next six months planning the stag night and fretting over his speech.

Pocket fact &

Torn between old pals and new best friends, grooms are increasingly choosing more than one best man and using each according to his strengths. This works brilliantly if one is a born organiser but a little shy and the other is a natural entertainer with a memory like a sieve.

BEST MAN'S DUTIES

- Helping sort out wedding transport, from booking cars to carry the bride and her father to the ceremony, and the couple after the ceremony, to taxis or lifts between the ceremony and the reception

- Going on shopping expeditions with the groom to hire/buy outfits

- Arranging the stag party, in co-operation with the groom, obviously, and being responsible for collecting deposits from the other stags, paying the balance for any accommodation or catering and checking the groom gets home with both eyebrows intact

- Being responsible for getting the groom to the ceremony on time (usually by putting him up at his own home so that the couple can spend the night before the wedding apart)

- To brief and co-ordinate the ushers

- Safely carrying the rings to the ceremony and producing them when asked by the official

- Giving the closing speech, usually laced with humour, never rude or insulting

- Acting as a master of ceremonies where necessary, making announcements to guests that drinks will be served in a certain room or dancing will start in 20 minutes etc

- Dancing with the chief bridesmaid (optional) after the newly-weds have started the evening off with their first dance

- Making sure the groom's overnight things are safely stored ready for the taxi to the first night hotel (or his honeymoon case, if they're going straight off on honeymoon)

- Settling any cash bills on the day on behalf of the groom, ie bar bill, taxis, tips

Pocket fact ✇

It was traditional to give the minister who married you odd rather than even money when you paid for the service. That's not so easy to do now that we pay for so much by debit cards, but maybe the best man could give the minister a donation to the church collection fund — say £10.01?

🐝 USHERS 🐝

Formal etiquette used to stipulate that there should be one usher for every 50 guests, but it really doesn't matter any more than it matters how many bridesmaids there are. Essentially ushers are the foot soldiers to the best man's commanding officer. If you have brothers, sons or nephews who are feeling a bit left out of arrangements, it's fine to have a few more providing you give them specific tasks and they don't all bump into each other at the back of the ceremony.

USHERS' DUTIES

- The main job is to co-ordinate the arrival of all the guests at the ceremony. This includes a welcome smile, giving out buttonholes where necessary, giving out orders of service or hymn books and gently reminding guests that they should switch off their mobile phones.

- Ushers traditionally ask guests which side they represent, ie bride or groom and indicate which side of the ceremony they should sit on. However, it's much more useful if ushers show people where to sit, ie keep the front rows free for close family. People are also inherently timid and will often fill up a ceremony from the back first, so your ushers should be looking for big gaps in the seating and encouraging guests to fill them.

- After the ceremony, it's always a good idea for the ushers to check under the seats or pews for forgotten cameras, gloves, confetti etc, especially if guests are moving on to another location for the reception.

🐝 FLOWER GIRLS AND PAGE BOYS 🐝

These little attendants are largely decorative and designed to draw a collective gasp as they enter your ceremony. It's enough for very small children to behave without being overwhelmed by the occasion, but older children can be given little tasks such as scattering petals along the aisle or carrying the rings on a cushion. Don't expect too much of little attendants as children have a low boredom threshold (see Common Wedding Problems pages 168–169).

Pocket tip 🥂

With very small children it's not always a good idea to take them to the ceremony rehearsal before the wedding. Standing in an imposing venue or an empty church can quite often freak them out. Under fives are not likely to remember what you tell them about where to stand anyway, so it's usually better to explain what is going to happen, have mum or dad hovering nearby when they enter the ceremony and let them experience the real thing in real time.

THE BLUSHING BRIDE: BECOMING A VISION

🌸 FINDING THE DREAM DRESS 🌸

The big white dress wasn't always associated with weddings. In fact until the 19th century, women got married in whatever colour they liked (or whatever colour they owned, depending on their finances). An old poem sets out the lucky colours associated with marriage clothes, of which white was one:

'Married in White, you have chosen right,
Married in Blue, your love will always be true,
Married in Pearl, you will live in a whirl,
Married in Brown, you will live in town,
Married in Red, you will wish yourself dead,
Married in Yellow, ashamed of your fellow,
Married in Green, ashamed to be seen,
Married in Pink, your spirit will sink,
Married in Grey, you will go far away,
Married in Black, you will wish yourself back'

Throughout the ages the unluckiest colour was always green – a bride in green was always considered a woman of 'ill repute'!

Pocket fact 💍

Queen Victoria was thought to be the first high-profile bride to choose white satin when she married Prince Albert in 1840. After that a long white dress became de rigueur, until the 1920s when fashion icon Coco Chanel designed the world's first knee-length wedding dress with a long train and anything became possible.

COUTURE OR HIGH STREET?

Buying a wedding dress (or a suit for the groom) can be a confusing business; there are so many terms to get your head around – bespoke, couture, made to measure, made to order, off the peg – although the deciding factor is usually budget.

Here is a quick run down of the common terms you'll come across when dress shopping:

Couture

Taken from the French term *haute couture* (high dressmaking) a couture dress was traditionally made from scratch – an entirely original design conceived by the bride and the designer and not dependent on an existing pattern. This is by far the most expensive way of buying a wedding dress although you will see the term couture used by companies that don't offer a couture service in the strictest sense of the word, so just make sure you get what you're paying for.

Pocket tip 🖑

If you've always dreamed of a designer dress, start looking around at least six months beforehand so that you have time to get in the right number of fittings – and time to save! But be realistic about weight loss plans and give yourself a cut off point, otherwise the dress could be hanging off you on the day.

Bespoke

This is a similar term to couture and tends to be used in connection with men's tailoring rather than dressmaking. The term itself came under legal scrutiny in 2008 when a complaint was made to the Advertising Standards Authority (ASA) against a tailor who was offering a 'bespoke' suit to an existing pattern and the ASA confirmed there was a lot of confusion within the industry itself.

Such was the confusion over the term bespoke (and its misuse), Savile Row Bespoke, an association set up in 2004 to represent

London's traditional Mayfair tailors, set out its own definition. It declared a bespoke outfit should be made to *'the customer's specifications . . . cut by an individual and made by highly skilled individual craftsmen. The pattern is made specifically for the customer and the finished suit will take a minimum of 50 hours of hand work and require a series of fittings.'*

Made to measure or custom-made

This is a half-way house between couture and off the peg, where you can choose an existing style of dress and then customise it to suit your style, ie change the neckline, add sleeves, change the strap style etc. It is then made from an existing pattern to fit your measurements with the customisations. It is not designed from scratch. Many bridal designers offer a range of styles where you can basically choose the skirt from one, and the bodice from another, and the sleeves from a third. Obviously this process is more expensive than buying off the peg but less costly than couture.

Pocket fact &

Most brides try on between 12 and 15 dresses before they find 'the one'.

Made to order

The Advertising Standards Authority consider both 'bespoke' garments and 'made to measure' garments to come under the more generic term of 'made to order'. In other words, they are made to the customer's precise measurements and specifications – you don't pick them off the rail in the high street and take them home with you the same day.

Off the peg

This is a dress which you can walk in off the street and buy. Although this is the cheapest option it is possible to customise a dress from a high-street chain to make it one of a kind, such as adding a sash or wearing a wrap.

 CHOOSING A STYLE TO SUIT

Check out three or four different bridal shops and research styles online so that you know the shapes and styles before you start trying on. But be prepared to try styles outside your comfort zone, especially if the sales consultant suggests it. They fit dresses all day and they know how to hide that bottom and flatter that waistline!

The main styles for wedding dresses are:

A-line or princess line

This has a half-full skirt (think a capital A) rather than a big ballroom skirt. Some start to flare from underneath the bust, others have more of a fitted waist, but this style is universally flattering, as it draws the eye away from a full waist and plays down big hips.

Ballerina or ball-gown

This has a fitted waist with a big, full skirt, often with several layers. The volume of the skirt can create curves on a boyish frame, but can also swamp a small figure. The big skirt also emphasises a small bust, so choose an embellished, decorative bodice rather than a plain one.

Empire line

This is high-waisted with a loose skirt which is straighter than a ballerina or princess style (think Elizabeth Bennett in *Pride and Prejudice*). It can hide hips and the high waist creates a sense of height but it also emphasises a big bust.

Mermaid

This is a figure-hugging style (think 50s Hollywood screen icons) with a fishtail at the back. Suits a curvy figure rather than a pear shaped one as its second-skin appearance will accentuate a pot belly or a flat bosom.

Column

The straightest of the bridal styles, classical Grecian style which can be unforgiving on plump or petite brides as it emphasises bottom and hips.

Bias cut

This design is cut across the grain of the fabric to make one continuous piece of fabric. Bias cut dresses cling to the body and can be super flattering on thin frames but unforgiving on lumps and bumps.

Pocket tip 🥂

Two's company, three's a crowd and four's a coach party! Take one trusted friend dress shopping who's going to be patient about your indecision. You want honest feedback about the dresses you like the look of, not more than one opinion. You can always take mum or a different friend for a second look once you have a shortlist.

Some points to remember when planning your bridal outfit:

- As Coco Chanel once said: 'Fashion fades, only style remains' so focus on classic styling rather than on-trend fashion designs.

- Choose a style because it suits *you*, not because it looks good on someone else.

- Subscribe to the 'less is more' theory. The first thing people should notice is a bride's sparkling eyes and big smile, not her over-powering choker, earrings, tiara and feather boa.

TRICKS TO DISGUISE A. . .

Thick waist

Choose a style with a low waist, that starts an inch or so below the problem area, and get some good supportive underwear. Look for a bodice with a V-shape at the bottom, as the V panel will disguise your tummy.

Big bust

The worst way to disguise a heavy bosom is to cover it up in a high neck. Go for a sweetheart, V-neck or bateau neckline and soften with lace or ostrich feathers. Or try a halterneck top, which works better for a full bust.

Generous bottom

Avoid fishtail styles which will just draw the eye to the problem area. Look for low waists rather than nipped in waists, which can give your bottom a parcel shelf look at the back.

Pocket fact 🍀

Almost half of all brides-to-be and over a third of their grooms consider having some form of cosmetic procedure before the big day. The report from www.goodsurgeonguide.co.uk found that 58% of engaged women were considering — in order of popularity — botox, teeth whitening, liposuction, breast augmentation or face plumpers. For their grooms, the priorities were veneers, botox, hair plugs, liposuction and chest reduction (moob jobs). And you thought crash diets were extreme!

🌸 A QUICK GUIDE TO FABRICS 🌸

Choosing a wedding dress can be a bit bewildering and much of the price will be determined by the fabric and how much hand-work the dress requires. In a nutshell, a pure silk dress is going to be expensive, a silk mix with a man-made fibre is going to be more affordable. Other materials you might come across include:

- **Shantung silk**: a medium-weight textured silk
- **Dupion silk**: a heavier silk
- **Duchesse satin silk**: a medium weight, glossier version of normal satin
- **Chiffon**: a light, floaty draping fabric (good for weddings abroad)
- **Tulle**: netting that's often used under a skirt to create the ball gown effect.
- **Organza**: a light finishing fabric that's often used for layering over full skirts

- **Crepe**: light and floaty fabric used for unstructured and bias-cut dresses (this light fabric is good for weddings abroad)

Pocket fact ❧

Twenty-five-year-old Lin Rong from north-east China swept into the record books with the longest ever wedding dress. It measured a staggering 2,162 metres, equal in length to 18 average football pitches! It took three hours for the 200 guests to unravel the dress's train covered with over 600 crystals.

❦ QUESTIONS TO ASK YOUR ❦ BRIDAL SHOP

Q: Are fittings included in the price and how many should I expect to have?

Q: Are any alterations (ie trimming the hem) included in the price and how much should I expect to pay for others?

Q: When do I have my last fitting – an important question if you're trying to trim down and also because brides often drop weight in the last couple of weeks because of nervous energy

Q: When can I collect the dress?

Q: What is your cancellation policy, how much is the deposit and when does the balance have to be paid?

Q: Does the price include VAT?

Pocket tip 🥂

Don't just bowl up to a bridal shop on a Saturday, as they probably won't have time to serve you properly. Make an appointment or, better still, go during the week. Try to order a made to measure dress at least six months before the wedding. If you leave it too late, ie three–four months before, there may be an 'express' or 'rush' charge added to the bill, especially if the dress is being made abroad.

ACCESSORIES

VEIL

A veil is one of the most symbolic accessories at a wedding and one of the earliest things little girls associate with weddings, usually when they play act getting married with net curtains on their head! They're not mandatory for weddings, although some more orthodox religions may prefer brides to have their heads covered, and certain styles go best with certain styles of dress.

Different lengths of veil

Cathedral

This is the longest variety that glides up the aisle behind you. It can measure up to a show-stopping 12 feet, and is usually worn at very formal weddings.

Chapel

Another long one, this veil should just skim the floor.

Princess

Sometimes called a **waltz** or **ballet** veil, this veil should fall just above the knee and is a good camouflage for big hips or bottom.

Fingertip, elbow or shoulder

These are all named after the section of the bride's figure where their length will fall and suit different dresses depending on the style.

Blusher

This is the shortest length which is usually worn full face and finishes beneath the jawline. These often work well on brides who are not wearing a long dress, but prefer a tailored suit.

Fascinator

Increasingly popular as a veil substitute, a fascinator is mid way between a hat/hair accessory and a veil but still offers a little netting veil for the bride to peep out.

Pocket fact 🕮

In the Jewish faith the custom of 'bedeken' is where the groom traditionally veils his wife before the ceremony. The custom is thought to date back to Biblical times and the story of Jacob, who was tricked into marrying Leah, rather than her sister Rachel, because she was hiding behind her veil.

SHOES

There's an argument that with a traditional long dress, no-one gets to see the bride's shoes. Try telling that to Britain's brides who spend hundreds of pounds on their big day footwear. The main thing to remember is they should be comfy – this is going to be a long day.

Pocket fact 🕮

Peep-toe bridal shoes, or shoes with strappy or cut-away sides, tend to be best for lasting the course as even the tiniest amount of air circulating around your toes keeps them cooled and comfortable.

Bridal shoes and lucky customs

1   In some cultures the bride's father would give the groom a shoe at the wedding which represented passing over responsibility for her future journey to the new husband. It could also date back to the Egyptians when a shoe was considered a symbol of fertility.

2   One old Swedish tradition involves putting coins in the bridal shoe. A bride would put a silver coin from her father in the left shoe and a gold coin from her mother in the right in the hope that she will never go short after she leaves the family home.

3   Traditionally brides believed their marriage would get off on the right foot if they paid for their wedding shoes with coins collected over the years.

4 Sprinkling salt into a bride's shoe was once thought to symbolise a prosperous future.

Pocket tip 🎍

If you're choosing a heel higher than the one you usually wear make sure that — combined with your glamorous wedding day up-do — you don't end up towering above your groom.

🌾 YOUR BRIDAL BEAUTY REGIME 🌾

A bride obviously wants to look her most gorgeous, in the flesh and in the photos, so get some tips and advice from a professional make-up artist beforehand, even if you don't actually have professional make-up on the day. Remember, you will need a little more make-up than usual, to bring out your eyes, shade your cheekbones and highlight your smile, but you don't want to look like a painted doll — because then you won't look like you and that's who your groom fell in love with!

Pocket fact 💍

Don't be shocked if your hairdresser suggests you wash your hair the day before the wedding and not on the morning itself. Day-old hair is often easier to work with and helps the stylist arrange your tiara or accessories without having to use too much heavy product.

BRIDAL BEAUTY DOS AND DON'TS

- Don't overdo the fake tan. A white or ivory dress will just makes it look even more orange. If you want a golden glow, have it applied professionally, a few days before the wedding and have a practice several weeks beforehand so that you know how quickly it fades, and whether it goes patchy.

- Do enhance features with a sweep of matt bronzing powder around the hairline and on the temples, jaw line and cheekbones.

But be very careful with bronzers and powders around the neck and décolletage as this can easily come off on your dress.

- Don't overdo glittery powders or bronzers as camera flash bounces off the reflective particles and can make you look sweaty.

- Do highlight eyelids with a soft pencil, even a little line of smoky grey or a very dark green, to give eyes definition, especially if you're going for a lot of black and white photography. Smudge it gently with a cotton bud after application if you're worried it looks too harsh.

- Don't go for a bright show-stopping red lipstick unless it's your usual look. It can overpower your smile and eyes and look harsh against your dress. And be cautions with the lip gloss. A little gust of wind and your hair or veil could easily become stuck on it.

- Do make-up touches in a warm environment as make-up doesn't glide on as well in a chilly room. Try warming foundations or creme blushers in your palm.

Pocket tip

If damp weather makes your hair go frizzy, a light slick of hand cream warmed in the palm of your hands and gently smoothed over your style can help the hair cuticles lie flat again.

WEIGHT LOSS FOR BRIDES

There are as many diet plans as there are days of the year but if your goal is to tone up for the big day, the best advice is do it slowly. The physical demands of planning a wedding, dealing with family politics and worrying about budgets can be draining on the immune system so you need to eat sensibly and make sure you get all the necessary minerals, vitamins and your 5-a-day. Skipping meals may help you drop a few pounds, but it will leave you with dull looking skin, lack-lustre hair and big bags under your eyes. Not a good look in the photos.

Pocket fact

The biggest worry among brides is the wedding arrangements themselves (63% lie awake at night worrying about the organisation) while around the same number of grooms are most stressed out about remembering to thank the bridesmaids and getting through their speech unscathed.

 DRESSING THE WEDDING PARTY

THE DASHING GROOM

Although the focus will be on the bride's dress, the groom will also want to look his best.

Finding the perfect suit

Traditionally weddings took place early in the day, so 'morning wear' was appropriately named. Today, the striped trousers with a tail coat, waistcoat with matching tie or cravat and top hat can be worn for weddings at any time of day, although as late afternoon weddings become increasingly fashionable, many couples are choosing black tie, which gives female guests the chance to wear evening gowns. Other popular occasion wear for grooms includes frock coats for the Edwardian gentleman look or even Highland wear. If there is a set dress code (ie tails), this usually extends to the ushers and family members on both sides, so make sure the boys approach a men's outfitters in plenty of time to make sure all the sizes you need are available. This is especially important for exceptionally big sizes and children.

Pocket fact

If your groom has Scottish connections but is unsure of his family tartan, he can look it up via the Scottish Register of Tartans. And if he does go for the Highland look, make sure he doesn't go all traditional and decide to be a 'true Scotsman' (wearing a kilt without underwear) in case the wind blows up and catches him unawares on the big day!

OUTFITS FOR THE BRIDESMAIDS

Getting bridesmaids to agree on a design that you and they like is one of those hurdles that many brides face (see Common Wedding Problems, page 170). And be careful if you're buying dresses off the peg in department stores and need a variety of sizes as they can be difficult to track down, especially at certain times of year when store space is needed for other things. (In December stock is minimal because of Christmas, and in January, July and August bridal wear is often sidelined by the sales.)

Pocket tip 🥂

If you are buying for younger bridesmaids, bear in mind that it can be hard to fit the 'tweeny age group' (10–12) as many children's sizes stop at age 10 and your rapidly growing teenage bridesmaids may have to go into adult sizing.

AFTER THE PARTY'S OVER

Congratulations you're married! You don't need to feel down now that the party is over though, there's still a lot more fun to come.

🐝 THE WEDDING NIGHT 🐝

One wedding tradition that has changed beyond all recognition is the first night. At one time, the happy couple would leave the party half way through the evening and change into travel-wear, known as going-away outfits. They would say their farewells, the bride would throw her bouquet and they would drive off on honeymoon with a few tin cans tied to the back of the car while everyone stayed behind to finish off the sherry.

Pocket tip 🥂

You have enough to do planning the wedding, so leave arrangements for the first night to the best man and chief bridesmaid. They can make sure your overnight bags are delivered to the first night suite (either at the same venue as the party or have it taxied to your own hotel).

Today, couples are determined not to miss the biggest (and most expensive) party of their lives just to get stuck in traffic on the M25 to Gatwick. Most stay to the end, often in the same venue and there's a growing trend for the debrief brunch the next day – a chance for everyone to get together again (normally late in the morning) to nurse their hangovers, check out each other's digital pictures and swap stories of the day.

Pocket fact &

Grooms who want to wow their bride on the first night of their honeymoon should take a leaf out of Ross Frazer's book. Romantic Ross wrote to 300 famous people asking them to send new bride Louise their congratulations. Over 60 celebs replied with good wishes and signed photos, including ex US president Bill Clinton, Harry Potter star Daniel Radcliffe and rugby star Jonny Wilkinson!

🐝 THE HONEYMOON 🐝

Until the 1960s/1970s, few couples in the UK could afford to go anywhere glamorous for their honeymoon. They had a few days on the coast (the Isle of Wight was the height of sophistication!) and then it was back to the day job. Today, the honeymoon has taken on epic proportions, to the point where couples are increasingly asking guests to contribute to the travel fund via gift vouchers, tour operator gift list schemes or 'honeymoney'. For this reason, the tradition that the groom books the honeymoon as a surprise has gone a bit by the wayside. No modern bride wants to turn up at a five-star resort in the Indian Ocean with the wrong wardrobe!

THE MODERN 'HONEYMOON'

As we move beyond the traditional long weekend on the coast there are a number of new terms popping up to describe the honeymoon:

Minimoon

If your bank accounts are empty after the wedding, a budget-friendly, short-haul trip is one option just to mark the occasion, while you save up for the Seychelles or the Caribbean for your first anniversary, or Annimoon.

Annimoon

The big holiday you couldn't afford to take straight after your wedding, taken to celebrate your first anniversary.

Megamoon

This really is the trip-of-a-lifetime, with newlyweds taking off a month or more (or even taking a sabbatical) and heading off round the globe.

Voluntourism

If you feel the past few months have been a bit 'me, me, me' what about a honeymoon with a purpose, combining sightseeing to helping out on volunteering projects from India and the Philippines to Mexico and Brazil?

Pocket fact ∞

It's not all seduction and sunsets on honeymoon. According to a survey from one cruise operator, 46% of couples are most looking forward to activities such as sightseeing on their honeymoon which is why a multiple destination holiday is a good idea.

DREAM DESTINATIONS

Magical minimoons

Great romantic destinations you can get to in under four hours include:

- **Italy**: the cities of Florence, Venice and Rome for the culture, the Amalfi coast for touring and posing, Tuscany for total escapism and fab food and wine!

- The **Greek islands**: Mykonos or Santorini for chic style, Lefkas for sailing

- **Morocco**: combine a couple of nights in the exotic city of Marrakesh, then head to the cool Atlas mountains or the beautiful coast of Essouria

- **Slovenia**: one of Europe's unexploited gems with picture postcard scenery and historic culture intact

---

Money saver

After their wedding in Friends, Monica and Chandler argued for upgrades on their airline on the basis they were honeymooners. This actually happens more rarely than people think. Most airlines won't upgrade passengers unless economy class is full. However, it's worth advertising your newlywed status to everyone you meet, as you may get special treatment, a room upgrade or, at least, a glass of bubbly!

Luxury long-haul

Classic beach destinations include the **Caribbean, The Seychelles, The Maldives, Mauritius** (which can be combined with a safari on the African mainland), **Sri Lanka**, and **Tahiti and French Polynesia** (a long way to fly but a great stop off if you're heading for Oz or New Zealand).

Pocket tip 🕯

The bride's tickets and passport MUST be in the same name. If you're desperate to travel in your new married name, you can send off for a new passport up to three months before the wedding. However the passport will be post dated so you can't travel until after the wedding and some countries will not issue visas for post-dated passports so check with the country's consulate first.

Know your time zones

If you're flying off straight after the wedding, think about local time when you arrive. The last thing you want to do after the most exhilarating time of your life is travel overnight and still arrive in the pitch black when everything is closed.

- **Heading west for the USA or the Caribbean?** *US east coast cities such as New York, Miami and Caribbean islands like Jamaica are 5 hours behind London, Mexico City is*

6 hours behind and Los Angeles or Las Vegas are 8 hours behind.

- **Heading for the Middle East?** Cairo is 2 hours ahead and Dubai is 4 hours ahead.
- **Heading south?** South Africa is 2 hours ahead of London, Kenya is 3 hours ahead, Casablanca in Morocco is the same time as London.
- **Heading east?** Sri Lanka and India are 5 and a half hours ahead of London, Bangkok in Thailand is 7 hours ahead, Singapore is 8 hours ahead.

Stress buster

Once you reach your dream destination, beat jetlag with a few drops of an uplifting citrus oil like lemon in your bathwater.

WHERE'S BEST WHEN?

Caribbean

The guidelines vary from island to island as they are spread over quite a distance. Generally speaking, the busiest (and most expensive) time to go is during the UK winter (Dec–March). The hurricane season is between July and November which doesn't mean you'll get them, just that there is a higher chance!

Mauritius

The western and northern areas tend to be warmer and relatively drier than the east and the south. Mauritian summers (November to May) are hot and dry and February is the warmest month. December to March is best for diving.

The Seychelles

These islands have a fairly constant temperature throughout the year, although tropical rains are more likely in January and February. April–May and October–November are the best times for snorkelling and diving.

The Maldives

December to April is the drier season. May to November is still hot, but can be more humid and has more rainfall.

Thailand

November to March is the best time to visit most of Thailand as it is less rainy and humid. April to June can get very hot, although temperatures are less extreme in the south.

Pocket fact ✿

For actor Sir John Mills the real star of the show was always his beloved wife Mary Hayley Bell. So much so that he celebrated every anniversary of their 64-year-long marriage by wearing the faded blue and white check jacket he first wore on their honeymoon in 1941! The couple were originally married at a quickie civil ceremony at a sandbagged Caxton Hall during the Second World War. Sixty years later, in 2001, the couple renewed their vows at St Mary's in Denham, Buckinghamshire.

HAPPY MEMORIES

PHOTOS

Unless you managed to see an early selection of your photos on the day (some photographers will have them available to view on a laptop at the reception), the big excitement coming back from honeymoon is choosing all the photos. These days this is usually done digitally rather than the old paper proof process.

The photographer will usually edit out the shots that didn't work and load the rest onto his/her website giving you a user name and password so that you can view the photos online and choose the images you want for your album. This way friends and family can order any shots they like directly from the photographer.

Pocket tips 🥂

If you put disposable cameras on the tables for guests to take fun pictures, at least one will go missing, they always do. Give the job of collecting them up and having them processed to someone reliable. But ask them not to make the prints or CDs available for general view until you've seen them first.

VIDEOGRAPHY

If you're having an official video, a rough cut should be edited and ready to view by the time you come back from honeymoon, unless the videographer has already told you there will be a delay. Couples are rarely involved in the edit; simply because it's your wedding and you'd never be able to decide what to leave out!

🌸 DELIVERY OF GIFTS 🌸

If you've registered with a gift list service, once you're back you can chase delivery. As fun as it is opening boxes of wonderful new things, pay good attention to the condition of things as you unwrap them. Check glassware is intact, lamps work and mirrors have not been scratched in transit. It's much easier to call up about a problem straight away. The same goes for substitute presents. If something has been delivered that is not the exact specification you asked for it could be that the line has been discontinued.

🌸 THANK-YOU CARDS 🌸

And with the gifts come the thank-yous. Try to make a note of who gave what so that you can mention it in your thank-you card rather than just saying something generic about 'the gift'.

3 WAYS TO MAKE YOUR THANK-YOUS UNIQUE

1. Take it in turns to photograph each other opening all the presents then send a pic of you opening auntie Jemima's slow cooker along with auntie Jemima's thank-you card.

2. Choose a favourite wedding photo of you both and use it as your thank-you card. If you can't afford to have them especially printed, get someone clever on the computer to design a fun newsletter using the picture that you can email to everyone, just substituting the name at the top and the details of the present in the text.

3. Ask your photographer to take a picture of you with every guest (or couple) along the receiving line (this works best with fairly small weddings of 50 or less), and send it with your thank-you note. If you don't have time, space or budget to do this with everyone, at least do it for the key players in the bridal party, groom, ushers, mums, sisters etc. A personal touch is always appreciated.

Pocket fact ✿

The post-wedding blues. A 2009 survey conducted by Yakult of 3,000 newly married brides revealed that a quarter felt so deflated after their big day was over, that they turned to comfort eating and piled on a stone and a half during their first year of marriage! Worse still one in five admitted that gaining the extra weight made them feel tetchy and led to rows with their new husband.

🐝 HAPPY EVER AFTER: WEDDING 🐝 ANNIVERSARIES

One year – paper	10 years – tin and aluminium
Two years – cotton	11 years – steel
Three years – leather	12 years – silk and linen
Four years – fruit and flowers	13 years – lace
Five years – wood	14 years – ivory
Six years – sugar and candy	15 years – crystal
Seven years – wool and copper	20 years – china
Eight years – bronze	25 years – silver
Nine years – pottery	30 years – pearl

35 years – coral

40 years – ruby

45 years – sapphire

50 years – golden

55 years – emerald

60 years – diamond

Pocket fact ❧

German psychologists claim that people who kiss their husband or wife every morning live an average of five years longer than those who can't be bothered to pucker up!

COMMON WEDDING PROBLEMS (DON'T WORRY, YOU'RE NOT THE ONLY ONES!)

❧ SHOULD WE INVITE CHILDREN, ❧ THEY ARE REALLY PUSHING UP OUR NUMBERS?

If you're on a tight budget and your guest list includes a lot of youngsters, you might have to take a deep breath and reconsider. Don't invite lots of children you don't know well for fear of offending their parents. You do the maths. If you're inviting eight couples from work with two children each and your food price per head is £30, that's nearly £500 of your budget to include 16 children you've never seen before. Each of your couples only has to find a fraction of that for babysitters!

> *Pocket tip* 🥂
>
> *If you're aiming for a chic cocktail party feel, maybe in a modern hotel or gallery, and you're not going down the traditional disco route, there may be nothing for the kids to do but get bored and whinge — then no-one has a good time.*

POSSIBLE SOLUTION

If you're saying no children, let parents know long before the invitations go out using phrases like, 'I hope you'll have enough time to find child care arrangements as we'd love you to join us on our big day. . .' Leave no room for compromise.

🐝 HOW DO WE KEEP CHILDREN 🐝 QUIET DURING THE CEREMONY AND ENTERTAIN THEM AT THE RECEPTION?

Crying children can't be helped but you don't want to be drowned out while trying to say I do. Similarly there's nothing worse than children moaning they're bored while the groom tries to express how much he loves his new wife.

POSSIBLE SOLUTION

At the ceremony it's madness to sit a baby with their parents in the middle of a front row during the ceremony. If the baby plays up, the embarrassed parents have to clamber over everyone like leaving the cinema in the middle of a film! Brief your ushers to seat little ones at the end of rows. You can also check to see if your venue has a special soundproof children's area which allows parents to still see what's going on but means you don't have to hear the little ones!

6 TIPS FOR HAPPY CHILDREN AT WEDDINGS

1. Most children don't like terrines or salmon so ask your caterer for a simple pasta dish or chicken breast. Better still, see if they will make them up a picnic box.

2. A wedding can be a long day for children so punctuate the day with some form of entertainment if the budget will run to it. A magician or balloon artist can give them something to look forward to (and for parents to use as a bribe to keep them quiet during the ceremony and speeches).

3. Children have real energy boosts and lulls, often linked to their blood sugar levels, so think about timings. It may help to feed them earlier than your adult guests.

4. Before the ceremony children are usually overawed by the spectacle and the bride's arrival, but 10 minutes later when everyone has to be quiet for the serious business of the day, they can start to get fractious. Get your ushers to keep some seats or pews near the back for guests with small children.

5. If you're seating all the children on one table, think about the ages of the children involved. Under fives probably need to be with mum and dad and teenagers may not be impressed at sitting with youngsters, especially if you're expecting them to take responsibility.

6. Creche services can be useful if you want everyone to relax. Make sure they are Ofsted registered.

Pocket fact &

Some officials are more tolerant about children than others. In 2008, newlyweds Ashley and Vicky Thorpe of Stoke-on-Trent complained to their local diocese when their vicar halted their wedding mid-ceremony. The Reverend David Cameron objected to the couple's two-year-old son repeating the groom's name and asked for someone to remove him from the church. When the groom's granny defended the child, saying he wasn't causing any trouble the vicar asked her to leave too!

🐝 MY MOTHER (OR GROOM'S 🐝 MOTHER) IS TRYING TO TAKE OVER

Half the battle of planning a wedding is delegating tasks you don't want to do to the people who are willing to do them. You may also succumb to 'mum envy' when one of the mothers thinks the other is having too much say in the arrangements and feels left out. Try not to get annoyed, a little compromise can go a long way.

POSSIBLE SOLUTION

She may just want to feel involved, so rather than trying to keep mum at arm's length, find a couple of tasks that will keep her occupied, such as researching gifts for your attendants or pricing up favours – things that will take up a lot of precious time that you may not have.

🦋 I DON'T LIKE THE BEST MAN 🦋

If it's not nipped in the bud early, this can easily escalate to a stand-off position – it's him or me – which is not a realistic solution. Would you really jeopardise your future because you don't like the man standing beside your future husband?

POSSIBLE SOLUTION

If he didn't discuss his choice with you beforehand (some grooms get carried away and ring their best mate before thinking it through) you need to tackle him about it. BUT, don't say you don't like the best man, explain what it is that worries you, ie he's a bit scatty and might lose the rings or he gets a bit overexcited and could give a rude speech. Hopefully the groom will see your point and you can try to reach a compromise.

🦋 MY BRIDESMAID IS NOT DOING 🦋 HER BIT TO HELP

Twenty-first century bridesmaids have rather different demons to face – not least the best friend who turns into bridezilla. A 2008 survey by *You & Your Wedding* revealed that one in five brides would consider asking their bridesmaids to sign some form of contract (an innovation that started in the United States) to make sure they toe the line. On a positive note the most popular things brides wanted their attendants to do was be supportive on the day; turn up to all the relevant dress fittings and wear the dress the bride chose for them. However, the more extreme requests among over a thousand brides included asking bridesmaids:

- Not to outdo the bride (51%)

- Not to dramatically change their hair in colour or style (40%)

- Not to gain more that 7lbs before the wedding (25%)

- Not to make advances towards inappropriate male guests at the reception (19%)

🌿 I'M FEELING OVERWHELMED! 🌿

ABC OF KEEPING SANE

Appreciate what you have rather than what you don't have. So what if you can't afford two Lamborghinis and three weeks in the Maldives? You still have one Limo and a weekend in Madrid.

Back down over things that are not important to you. Only risk causing waves if it's something that you'll look back on and regret for years to come. Your flower girl wants a pony tail, you'd pictured plaits – does it really matter?

Compromise if one of you is set on one thing (he wants a chocolate fountain, you want a string quartet) have both, or have neither. There are no losers in this equation – you are both winners.

Delegate jobs to people who want to help and who will soon tell you if they don't have time. Give out jobs that can't really be done wrong – like collecting things from shops, researching, tracking down shoes in odd sizes – and keep all the decision making to yourselves.

> *Pocket tip*
>
> *Chill out, it's not life or death, it's a wedding. Most guests look back and remember the good stuff. And they're all your friends, so they want you to succeed!*

🌿 WHAT DO I DO WITH MY DRESS? 🌿

Whatever you do with it, make sure someone arranges for it to be professionally treated first even before you're back from honeymoon. Warn mum against dabbing stains before she takes it to the cleaners too, as this often spreads the stain and stops the professional from doing a good job.

Pocket fact 🕮

According to a survey by Oxfam, 82% of brides hang on to their dresses after their celebration even though they're not sure why.

SELL, STORE OR ADAPT

Donate it to – or wear it for – charity

A quick look on the internet reveals lots of charities who can turn your precious gown into well-needed funds. Or why not raise money and have some fun by joining in with – or starting your own – fundraisers? Just like any other fundraiser, except everyone pays to wear their old dress again.

Have it dyed/made into something else

Check this is going to work before you go full steam ahead. Some materials are more porous than others so if your dress is made of more than one type of fabric, it may have to be pre-treated. It may simply just not be suitable for dyeing. Also remember that certain fabrics will shrink in the high temperatures needed to dye them.

Treasure/trash the dress

Away from the pressures of the big day itself, some brides like to put on the most expensive dress they ever bought one last time and get some glamorous magazine style images taken. There's also a trend for trash-the-dress shoots (the idea started in America) where brides put on their beloved gown one last time and pose for pictures totally at odds with the usual bridal pose – eg up a tree, rolling in a barn, under a waterfall.

To the world you may be one person, but to one person you may be the world.
Bill Wilson

INDEX